Analysis within the systems development life-cycle

Introduction

When I first began writing on this subject, I thought I would probably produce one book. Having collected the material together and organised it, I began to realise that it would be better as two and could logically become two. Now, having finished writing the first two books, I have realised that what at first was going to be one book about analysis is going to be four. The reason that one book grew into four lies in the objectives I set myself at the beginning. I decided that to be useful, the 'book' must provide the following:

1 *A comprehensive, even definitive, work on the subject of analysis:* I wanted to make sure I had covered the subject in such depth that a person wanting to analyse a system would not have to refer to other books because I had skipped a subject. It had to be the sort of book that could become a standard reference guide to the subject.

2 *A complete guide to all the deliverables that need to be collected in analysis:* I wanted the list of deliverables to take into account that we are not just carrying out an analysis for systems design purposes but that there may be deliverables we use for strategy studies and feasibility studies, as well as an extremely important set needed for such activities as hardware planning, software evaluation and organisational planning and design.

3 *A guide to the purpose of those deliverables:* I wanted to make sure that analysts realise that the facts collected—the deliverables—depend on the purpose to which they are going to be put. If the analysts are being asked to evaluate software, they will collect a different subset of facts from those needed for, say, hardware planning or database design. This meant that every time I described a deliverable, I needed to explain its purpose and emphasise that the list of deliverables had to be treated as a list of options.

4 *A book on deliverables, not on the myriad ways they could be packaged:* I wanted to emphasise this difference in the strongest terms. Nowhere in the four books will you find reports, forms, or data dictionary record layouts described as deliverables—because they obviously are not. They are means of packaging deliverables and an almost infinite number of packaging options exist. My message is forget about how you are going to package the deliverables when you have collected them, concentrate on *what it is* you are collecting and why you are collecting it, that way you are more likely to produce good results. You can decide on your packaging—the forms you want to design, the data dictionaries you want to adapt or build yourself—according to the list of deliverables which these mechanisms have to support.

5 *A book which offers a number of alternative ways of collecting the deliverables:* I wanted to give analysts a number of alternative, proven and up to date ways of collecting, analysing and verifying the deliverables, showing how the 'raw input'—for example, interview notes, or observation jottings—could be collected and then converted into the facts needed. Having carried out numerous projects, I recognised that reliance on one method was exceedingly dangerous and short-sighted. It is not always possible to interview people using 'top-down' methods and sometimes you have no existing design from which to work 'bottom-up'. The arguments about which methods are 'best' are pointless and very silly. There is no such thing as

'best'. Some methods are good in certain circumstances, some in others. Therefore, I concluded that I must discuss each of the methods with which I have experienced success, describing *when* they can be used, as well as their advantages and disadvantages.

These are the reasons why one book has ended up as a series of four. The books have been organised according to their objectives. The first split is based on the two main topics, which are:

1 The deliverables—what they are and their purpose.
2 The methods which can be used to obtain the deliverables, their advantages and disadvantages.

The next split is based on the logical split which occurs in the deliverables during analysis. The analyst concentrates on finding out the following two types of fact:

1 What data is needed to support the business activities.
2 What the business activities actually are.

The books, therefore, have been further split according to these two types of fact and you will, from now on, read the terms 'data analysis' and 'activity analysis'.

These are not separate 'techniques' as some people claim. Analysis is still one task, producing sets of deliverables related to 'activities' and sets of deliverables related to 'data'. The split is not a clean one and this will become obvious during the course of reading the books.

It is possible, however, to divide the books on this basis, while still keeping intact the concept of 'analysis' as one integrated activity. Thus the four books in the series are as follows:

1 'Data analysis—the deliverables'.
2 'Data analysis—the methods'.
3 'Activity analysis—the deliverables'.
4 'Activity analysis—the methods'.

This book, the first in the series, deals with the deliverables of data analysis. It describes all the facts—or more correctly types of fact—you need to collect about the data the business needs to support its activities. It does not discuss how these facts are collected or analysed. That is the subject of the second book.

The book has five chapters, organised as follows. Chapter 1 puts analysis into its place in the systems development cycle and explains what 'analysis' actually means. It also defines tasks such as 'hardware planning' and 'software evaluation' and where they fit into the overall cycle. This section is particularly important, as it explains both what it is we are trying to do and why we are doing it. Most of the time, the purposes listed by each deliverable are headed under the next 'logical' activities in the development cycle after analysis and you need to understand what is meant by them to be able to appreciate whether you have a need for that deliverable in your study. Chapter 1 also gives more detail about the importance of deliverables and why we should bother with them at all.

Chapter 2 introduces the main concepts which will be used throughout the rest of the book. They are concepts which are probably already familiar to a large number of readers but they are defined here, for completeness, and plenty of examples are cited. This chapter also introduces the main diagrammatic techniques that will be used to represent the deliverables. It does not matter what symbols are used, as long as they are used consistently. I have used one set throughout the four books and have introduced them in this chapter and shown what concepts they represent.

Chapter 3 is really for 'experts' and can be omitted if you do not know much about the subject yet. It describes important categories of concept. These categories are important because they represent classes which are distinct and special in the way they behave and the impact they have on systems. Really complex systems cannot be understood or analysed without using these different categories of concept. In fact, knowing that they are valid types helps a lot in the analysis process.

Chapter 4 deals with the real 'nitty-gritty' of this book. At this stage all the deliverables are described. It is the longest chapter in the book and is split according to main concept headings, that is what facts to collect about entity types, what facts to collect about attribute types and so on. There is also a section which deals with the deliverables of the *design* part of the systems development cycle. This is because one important set of analysis deliverables covers how the analysis deliverables have been *mapped* to the design deliverables. The major design deliverables are introduced but in the context of the need to record the mapping itself. No great detail is given.

Every deliverable listed under these major headings is followed by a description which covers the following four basic points:

1 The definition of the deliverable.

2 The purpose of each deliverable within the systems development cycle.

3 Diagrammatic conventions—how each deliverable can be pictorially represented, for example on the data model itself or separately as a matrix or histogram.

4 Hints and guidelines about the deliverable.

Finally, Chapter 5 summarises all the deliverables and then puts them into the context of the systems development cycle by describing the 'systems engine'—the 'meta-model' of the systems development life-cycle.

If you are an expert, you can read the book in the order given. While reading Chapter 4, you will find it interesting to refer to the subset of the systems engine—the meta-model provided in Chapter 5. If you are not an expert, read the book in the order given but miss out Chapter 3. After carrying out some analysis, you can refer back to this chapter for help. If you are an absolute novice, you may find it easier after reading the first two chapters to only skim through Chapter 4.

The book has been organised so that, once read, it can be used directly as a reference during any study of what needs to be collected and why you should be collecting it.

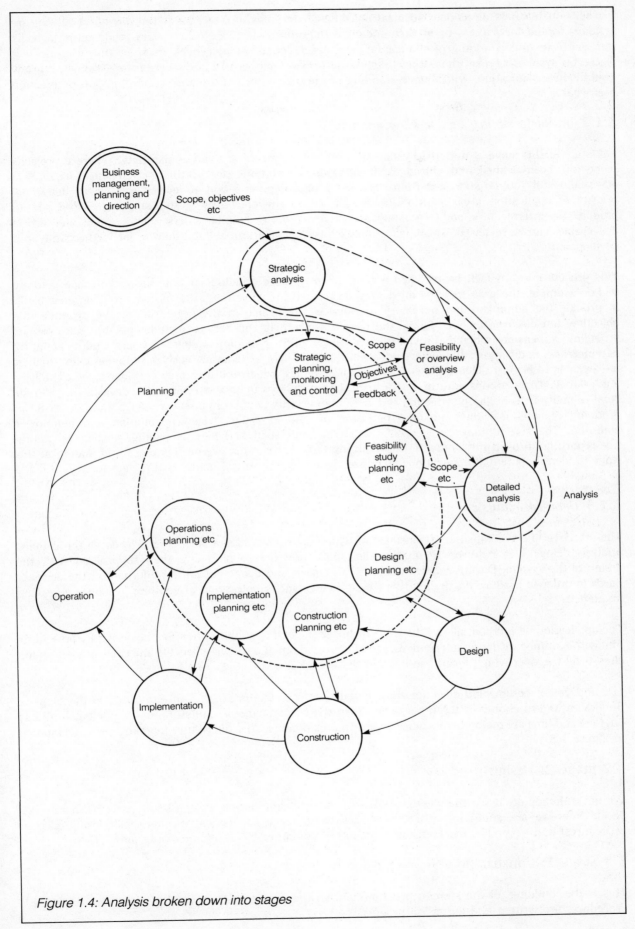

Figure 1.4: Analysis broken down into stages

9

it places on business directions, business objectives, key areas and targets at the director level. Future systems depend for success upon their match with future objectives, hence every study must logically start with an understanding of changes in business directions or objectives, in order that priorities are placed on systems to meet those objectives. Many projects fail because they were commissioned at a low level in the organisation, where understanding of the true nature of the business and its future direction was weak.

3.1.2 *Initial feasibility or overview analysis*

The start of this stage is initiated by the results from the strategic analysis planning, where a project's scope has been defined and objectives, budgets and limitations set for this second stage. The scope is usually still too large to determine feasibility or computerisation in every area or to determine priority of application areas within the overall scope. The objectives of this stage, therefore, are to produce an intermediary point in analysis, where feasibility can be assessed and costed and where deliverables can be reviewed. This application area is then split into suitable subsets for further study and development.

This process may, in fact, be repeated a number of times, depending on how large the scope actually is. For example, the area to be studied may be defined as 'personnel', the objective of this area being to provide the administration necessary to 'service' the people in the organisation. We examine this objective and discover that, as far as the user is concerned, this service includes paying those people, providing a pension scheme, providing medical services, providing welfare services and negotiating pay increases and improved benefits (industrial relations). As we examine each of these activities further, we are able to begin to identify logical groups of activities, which the user may consider to be of high or low priority. These groups and the importance the user places upon them help us to develop the plan for detailed analysis. For example, the first system of high priority may be 'manpower information', an artificial grouping of activities which includes provision of data for salary/wages negotiation and manpower planning. The second may be 'payroll', which includes such activities as paying people, calculating tax, reporting on overtime worked and submitting tax returns. Thus we need enough information at this stage to identify potential applications, expressed in terms of business activities, the data for which could be kept.

3.1.3 *Detailed analysis*

The objective of the detailed analysis stage, of which data analysis is a part, is to provide all the detailed analysis deliverables required to produce an application design plan and then to proceed with the design of the system. During detailed analysis, we collect and document all the information the designer needs in order to produce his design; this would include such information as volumes, response times and frequencies.

The application design plan allows the user to choose the best available option for the design by presenting him with a number of design alternatives, each one costed out and showing benefits and risks. It is the option chosen by the user which forms the basis of the actual design.

The application design plan does not show detailed design options; it aims only to establish the scope of the design and to choose between packages, 'own-written' systems or a mixture, on-line or batch and so on. Cost and time are major factors when producing the options. This 'alternative mapping' process is shown in Figure 1.5.

3.2 Stage 2: Design

We have already discussed the difference between analysis and design. Design is the process whereby we decide how we are going to satisfy the objectives in terms of 'clerical mechanisms' (forms, clerical procedures) and 'computer mechanisms' (computers, computer files, computer programs).

3.3 Stage 3: Construction

This is the 'building' of the system; programs are written and tested, physical files are created, clerical procedures are written and forms are produced.

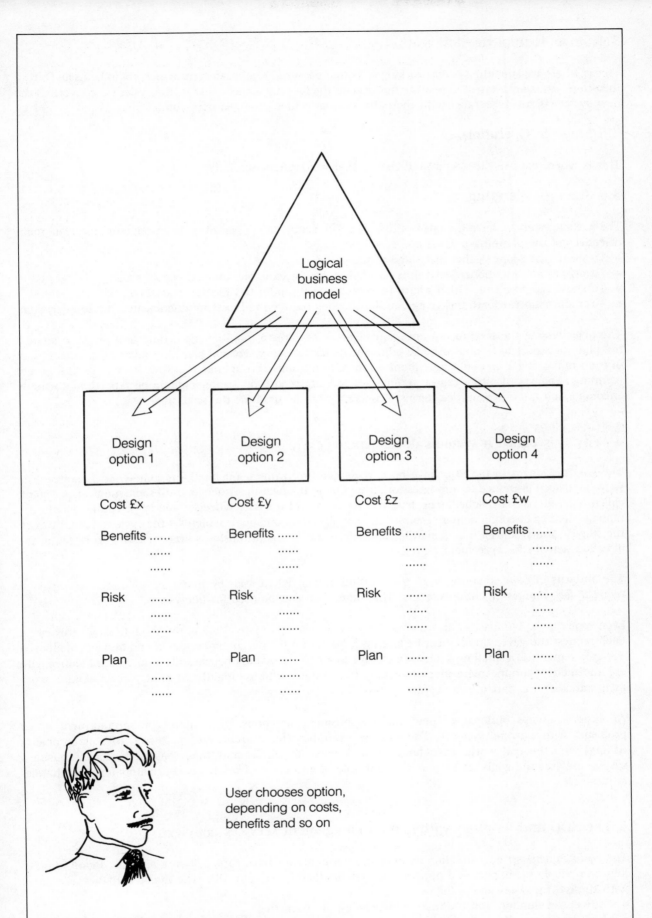

Figure 1.5: Application design planning

Chapter 2 Introducing the main concepts and diagrammatic techniques of data analysis

Chapter 2 Introducing the main concepts and diagrammatic techniques of data analysis

1 Introduction

This chapter is the starting point in describing the data deliverables, as it introduces, defines and gives examples of all the main concepts we will use from now on. There are four main building blocks used in data analysis. They are as follows:

1 The entity type.
2 The relationship type.
3 The attribute type.
4 The permitted value.

Of these four, the entity type and relationship type can be pictorially represented in a diagram known as a data model and the main diagramming conventions used in data or entity modelling are described later in this chapter. An additional, though less used pictorial technique, is described for the permitted values. Although it has a smaller role to play it is, nevertheless, a helpful tool. The chapter begins with a definition of the four building blocks.

2 Main concepts

2.1 Entity types

The starting point in our definition of an entity type is the 'entity', which is 'anything relevant to the enterprise about which information needs to be, or is, kept'. The main term used in data analysis is 'entity type'. This describes a group or classification of entities relevant to the enterprise which fit a given definition or description. The entity 'Rosemary Rock-Evans', for example, as far as the company DCE Computer Consultants Ltd is concerned, is an entity of the type 'consultant'. When activity analysis is performed it becomes clear that this definition is based largely on the activities of an organisation and how it views the classifications. In other words, the definition of an entity type and the classification of entities into types depends very largely upon context. In Figures 2.1 and 2.2, examples are given of some entities and entity types.

The analyst's most important tasks are the definition and identification of entity types.

2.1.1 *Synonyms*

Many people have shortened the term 'entity type' in general use to 'entity' and refer to 'entities' as 'entity occurrences'. This, unfortunately, can lead to confusion, for obvious reasons. As both entity types and

Entity types: Employee
                               Project

Relationship type: Works on

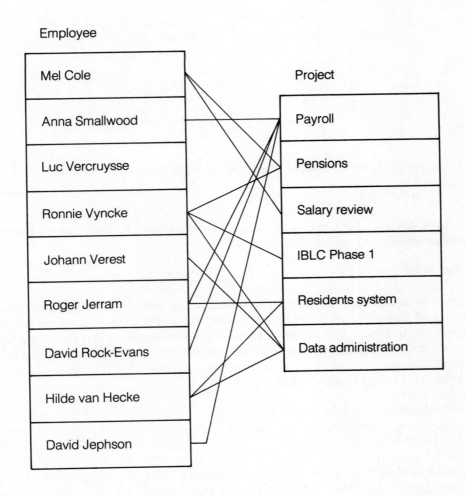

Figure 2.10: Many-to-many relationship (M:N)

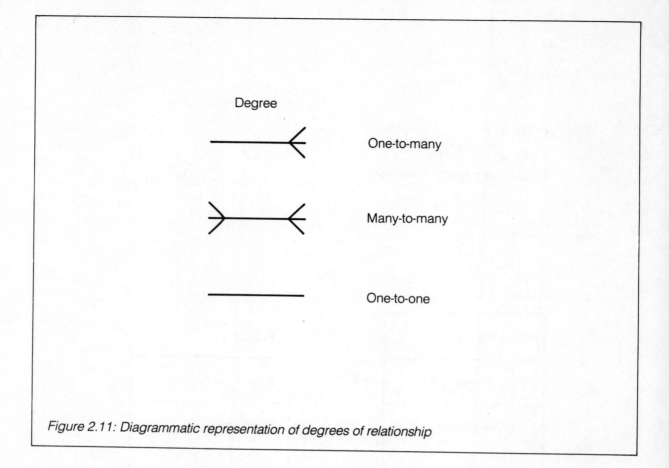

Figure 2.11: Diagrammatic representation of degrees of relationship

the individual facts known about the entity types Doctor, Clinic, Patient and Operation and their relationships are combined into one diagram.

3.2.3 *Involuted relationship types*

When an entity type is related to itself, the diagrammatic representation is called an 'involuted' data structure. Figure 2.14 shows the relationship type Doctor works with Doctor, which in this case is of the degree many-to-many. In Figure 2.15 another example is shown which, in this case, is one-to-many. We show what this means by using occurrences of the employee entity type. What we have is an *hierarchy* of command, that is;

- Smith supervises Levin, Brooks and Tweed
- Levin supervises Harris
- Brooks supervises Carter
- Carter supervises Rees, David, Fletcher and Stewart
- Fletcher supervises Palmer.

If we did *not* have a hierarchy but a 'network', we would have had to have a many-to-many relationship type. For example, Fletcher could have been supervised by many people (say Carter and Smith) and, in turn, could have supervised many people himself.

To help us establish the degree of relationships in the difficult 'involuted case', we should ask the same sort of question. Can an entity A have the relationship with many entity Bs in 'active' voice and with other entity Cs in 'passive' voice. For example:

	Answer
• Can Fletcher supervise many employees?	Yes
• Can Fletcher be supervised by many employees?	No.

In Figure 2.16, the involuted hospital relationship types have been added to the full model.

32

One-to-one relationship Type 1:1

Doctor

A doctor is in charge of one
clinic (and only one)

in charge of

Clinic

A clinic is the responsibility
of one doctor

One-to-many relationship Type 1:N

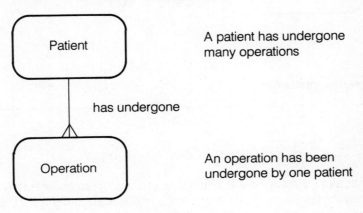

Patient

A patient has undergone
many operations

has undergone

Operation

An operation has been
undergone by one patient

Many-to-many relationship Type M:N

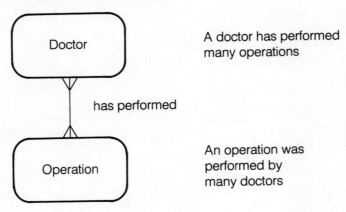

Doctor

A doctor has performed
many operations

has performed

Operation

An operation was
performed by
many doctors

Figure 2.12: Illustrating each degree of relationship

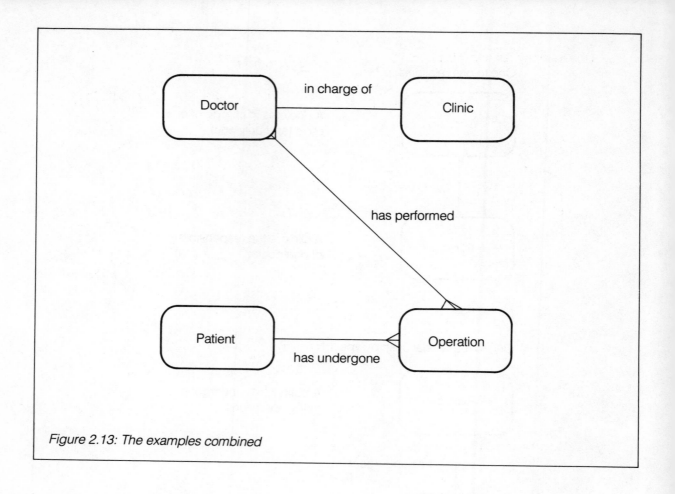

Figure 2.13: The examples combined

3.2.4 *Several relationship types between the same entity types*

If we have discovered that more than one relationship type exists between two entity types, we simply place the two (or more) between the two entity types. An example of this is given in Figure 2.17 which also shows occurrences, as follows:

1   Oughtibridge Hospital has Smith, Turpin and Bury registered with it but gave emergency treatment to Smith, Dick and Lyle.

2   Brightholmlee Cottage Hospital has Lyle, James and Tait registered with it but gave emergency treatment to Bury.

In Figure 2.18, these new facts have been added to the full model.

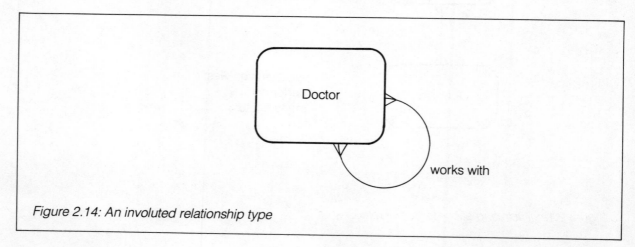

Figure 2.14: An involuted relationship type

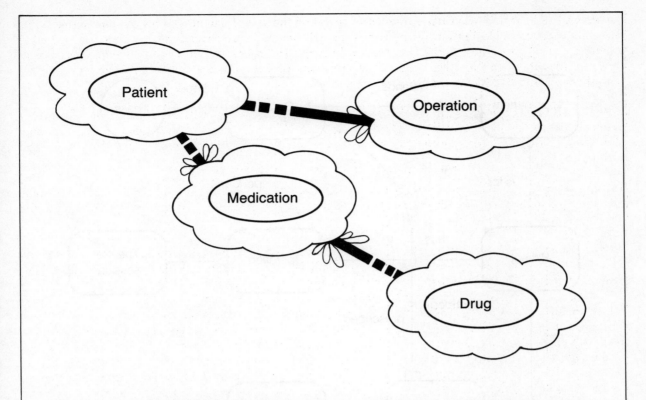

Figure 2.27: Other diagrammatic conventions are acceptable if they are clear, unambiguous and recognisable to other DP staff

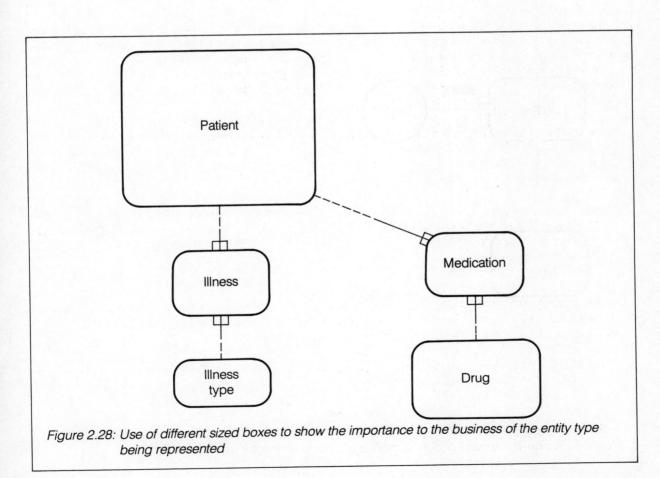

Figure 2.28: Use of different sized boxes to show the importance to the business of the entity type being represented

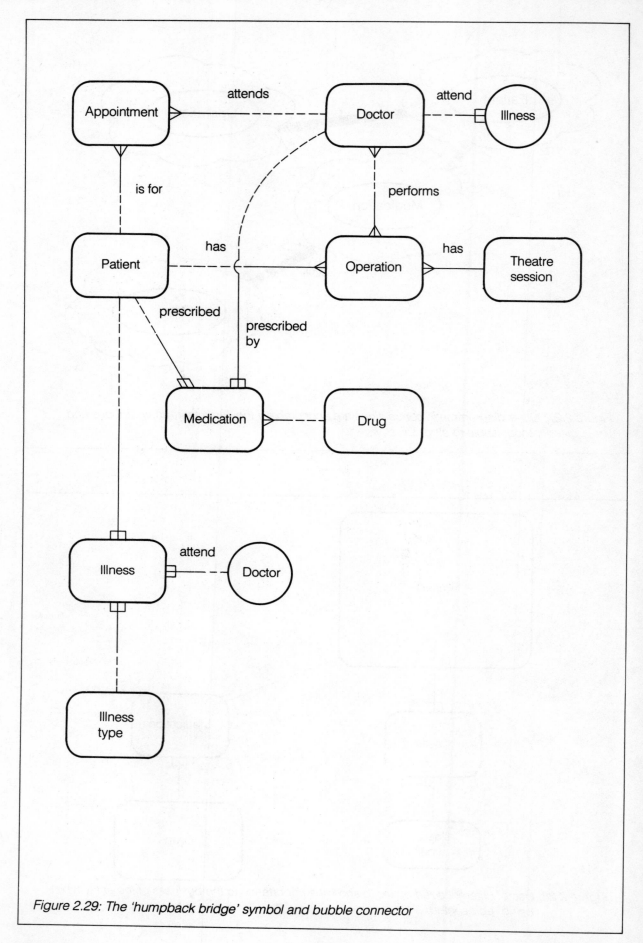

Figure 2.29: The 'humpback bridge' symbol and bubble connector

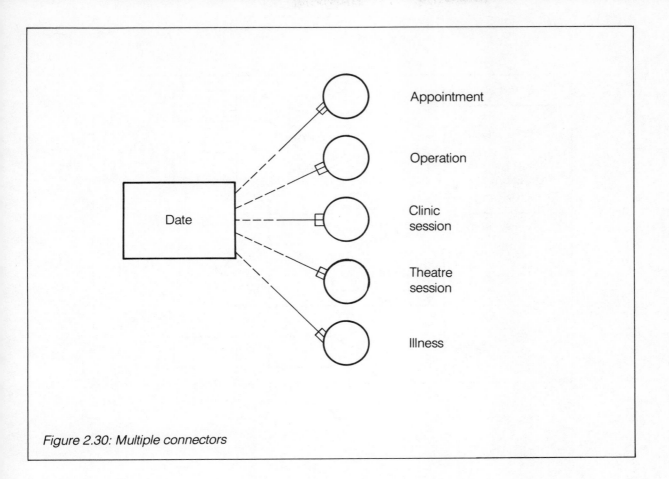

Figure 2.30: Multiple connectors

and a 'spaghetti junction' results, the same principle of connectors can be used. In this case multiple bubbles are created, one for each of the entity types the candidate entity type is related to (see Figure 2.30).

Where the entity type has a relationship with an enormous number of other entity types, then the bubble connector should be avoided. Instead the page can be ruled off, as shown in Figure 2.31, where one column is used for entity types having numerous relationship types with others. The bubble connector is then only used in the main model part of the diagram.

7 *Model detail:* during *detailed analysis*, the model is serving two purposes—communication with the user at a detailed level and communication with the designer. For the purpose of speaking with the user, a simplified model is best and no more extra detail should be added than is absolutely necessary. However, to help the designer, an 'overlay' model can be used, where some of the deliverables are written onto the model itself to help in design. An example of this is shown in Figure 2.32.

3.3 Types of model

There are three stages of analysis as follows:

1 Strategic.
2 Overview.
3 Detailed.

At the end of each of these stages a different model is produced as a deliverable. At the end of the strategic stage the 'fuzzy' model is produced; at the end of the overview stage, the 'overview' model; and at the end of the detailed stage, the 'detailed' model.

The change taking place in the model is simply one of refinement, based on the extent of knowledge.

The scope at the strategic analysis stage is broken down into five application areas, having their scope defined in terms of data and activities to be studied. Each is given a priority for further study.

During overview analysis the scope is further decomposed. These smaller application areas defined by the scope set in overview analysis are then studied during detailed analysis, the scope being broken down once more before design into 'subsystems'.

At each milestone point the scope - expressed in terms of data and activities to be studied - is a major deliverable passed to the next stage.

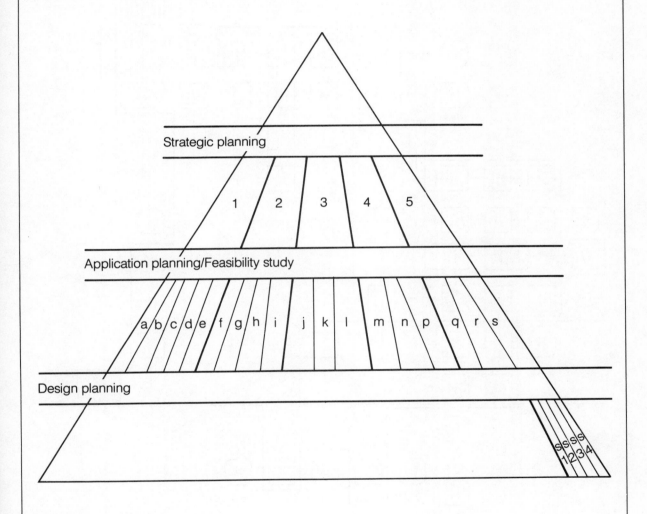

Figure 2.40: Progressive planning

The scope of the phase has been shown by drawing a line round the model relevant to that phase. Where data is shared it can be shown by an 'inset' line, an example of which is shown. Links with other entity types in other phases are shown by the bubble connector – the name of the entity type is written in the bubble and the bubble is placed outside the scope line.

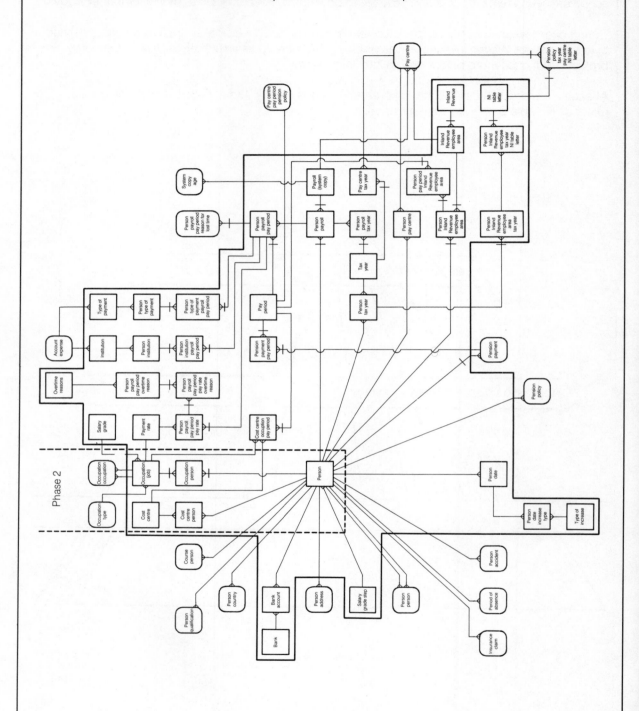

Fig 2.41: Phase 1 – 'Payroll'

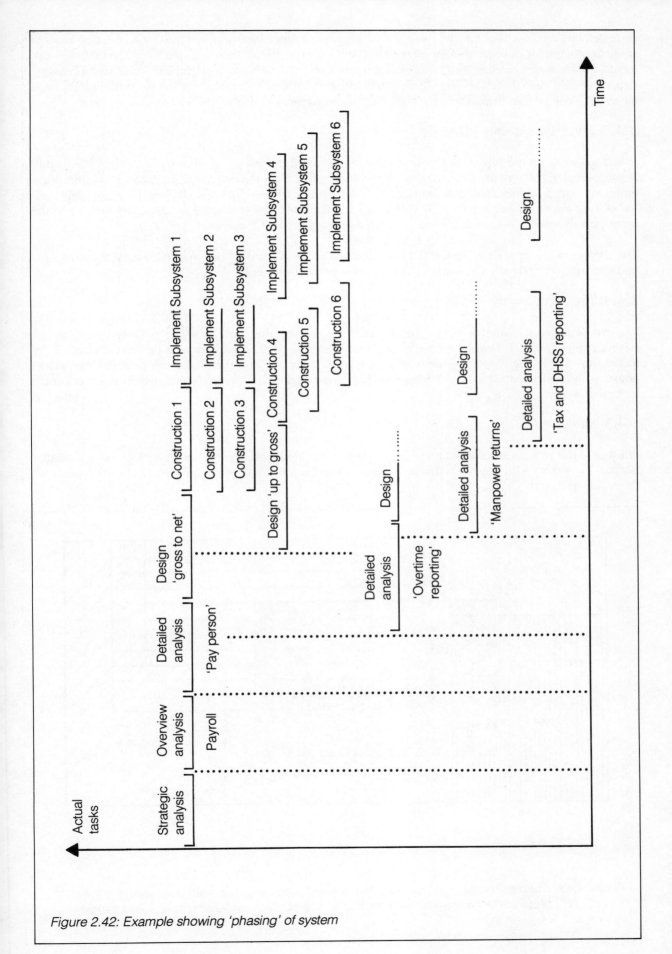

Figure 2.42: Example showing 'phasing' of system

61

Stage	Analysis	Design	Construction and implementation
Level	Conceptual	Logical	Physical
Elements	Entity	Record	Block
	Relationship	Segment	Data set
	Attribute	Set	Disk
		Data item	Tape
Symbols	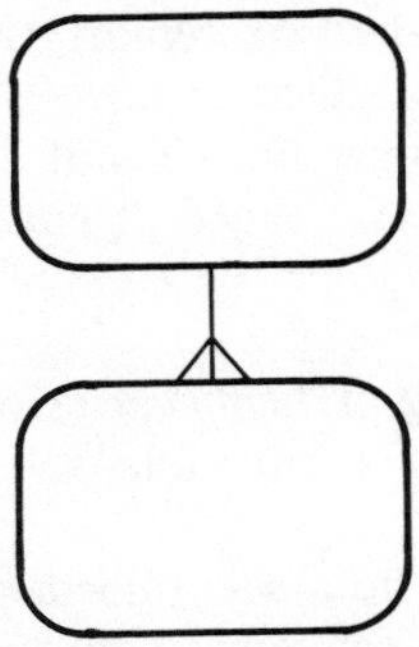	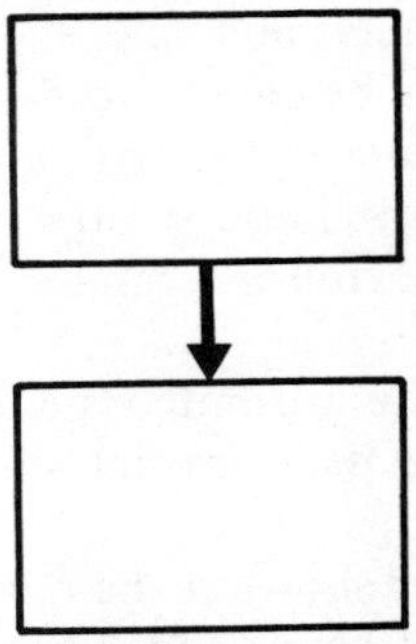	
Responsibility	Business analyst	Database and systems designer	Database designer
	Users	Applications programmer	Systems programmer
Example	Customer	01 BB-CUST-NAME	T...ABLE.........1,AC
		02 BB-CUST-INIT PIC X(4)	ACIA-AVENUE....U...BA
	Customer name	02 BB-CUST-SURN PIC X(15)	KER........2,ACACIA-A
		01 BB-CUST-ADDR PIC X(20)	VENUE....ETC
	Customer address		

Figure 2.49: Three levels of modelling

The limitations of the model must be realised, however. It cannot represent all the detail we collect. Its purpose is as a tool for summarising and a communication tool for discussion—a summary of what the enterprise is interested in and what it needs in order to operate. We must use the other methods to record the rest of the detail.

4 Additional diagrammatic technique—'entity life-cycles'

4.1 Introduction

Entity modelling as a diagrammatic technique is used to represent entity types and relationship types pictorially. The main drawback to the model is that it cannot show the 'dynamics' of the model or how it changes over time with respect to events. However, this can be done by using a diagrammatic technique known as the entity life-cycle diagram which represents the dependency between the permitted values of one attribute type of one entity type. It is only relevant to attribute types which are being used to describe events or activities and is only relevant when a history of events and activities is not required.

For example, the patient entity type may be single, then marry, divorce, remarry and then be widowed. The attribute type 'marital status' may be chosen to describe these different *exclusive* 'states', but where a history is required the attribute type 'marital status' would no longer be relevant and the attribute types date married, date divorced, date widowed and so on may be chosen instead. Event and activity recording attribute types are discussed in more detail in Chapter 3.

Entity life-cycles are only used when the attribute type is recording *mutually exclusive events*, that is events which can act on an entity type but which are not 'concurrently' permissible.

The diagram itself is not only useful for showing the dynamics of the model (albeit in a very limited way); it is also a useful checking tool as it can be used to determine whether events have been missed or whether an error has been made in assuming that events were 'exclusive' when, in fact, they are 'concurrent'.

The other use of the diagram is in validation, as it shows the basic validation rules which apply for an attribute type.

4.2 Diagrammatic conventions

The entity life-cycle diagram uses a circle to denote each permitted value representing an event or activity. An arrow is used to show what changes are allowed between permitted values. If there is a 'final' permitted value which represents the last event in the life of the entity, a double circle can be drawn. The one or more values which can 'start the life' of the entity can be shown by using a broad arrow (see Figure 2.50).

Several examples follow which demonstrate the technique. The first (see Figure 2.51) shows the entity type 'appointment' and the attribute type 'appointment status' which has the following permitted values:

- Booked
- Broken
- Cancelled
- Kept
- Archived.

After the first permitted value (booked), the appointment can be cancelled *or* broken *or* kept. From these values it can then be archived. Notice that the diagram shows that an appointment cannot be broken and then rebooked, or kept and then cancelled—it defines the permissible sequence of events and, hence, the change of all permitted values.

The next two examples show the entity type 'patient'. The first diagram (Figure 2.52) describes the attribute type 'marital status' and the next (Figure 2.53) describes the attribute type 'hospital status'. The point to note about both these is the way in which the entity can change permitted values in a repetitive fashion, for example married, widowed, married, widowed and so on. There does not have to be a progression from one value to the next, the cycle can be reversed.

Figure 2.53 not only illustrates how two entity life-cycles are applicable for the one entity type, but it demonstrates how, even when it is archived (which is effectively the end of its life), an entity type can still be *returned* to 'active' life by re-referral or an emergency which means the patient is admitted directly.

72

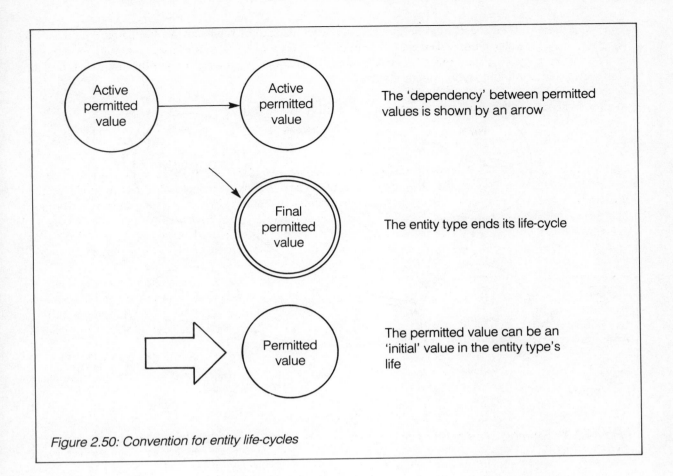

Figure 2.50: Convention for entity life-cycles

The 'dependency' between permitted values is shown by an arrow

The entity type ends its life-cycle

The permitted value can be an 'initial' value in the entity type's life

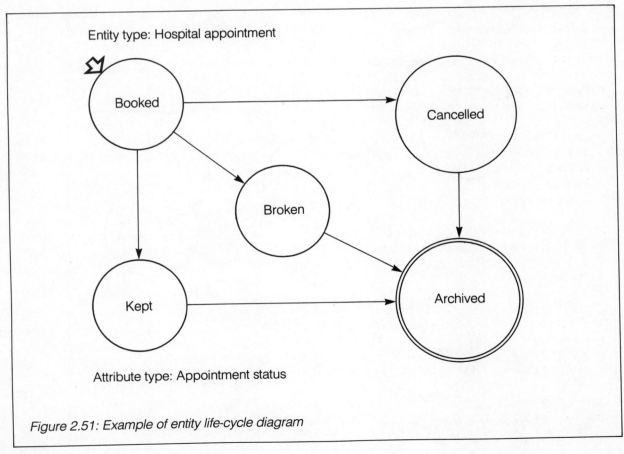

Entity type: Hospital appointment

Attribute type: Appointment status

Figure 2.51: Example of entity life-cycle diagram

The reason why multilevel classifications should always be represented as entity types is because they are hierarchical in nature. If we make this form of classification into an attribute type we have to make the structure into a fixed length block code as follows:

99	999	99
Broad	Intermediate	Detailed
Classification level	Level	Level

In this example we have had to fix the broad level to 100 possible categories, the intermediate to 1000 within each broad category, and the detailed to 100 within each intermediate level category. If we change this categorisation we have to change the format and this can cause severe disruption in a system which has been implemented.

A classification should be expansible and flexible to changing requirements, allowing expansion of categories without the need for excessive alteration in the system. We could build in an enormous safety margin when we invent the format, but this wastes space.

How should classifications be represented? The choice of representation is dependent on the *number* of classifications which are classifying our entity type and the flexibility required. Although a classification only classifies one entity type, it is possible that an entity type be classified in more than one way. Also, during analysis, the user may say that he is uncertain how he wishes to classify the entity type and he wants the facility to add *more* classifications in the future.

When only one or two classifications exist and there is unlikely to be any need for future expansion, the model shown in Figure 3.4 should be used. This shows a simple hierarchical structure of classes with the entities of the entity type being classified and linked to the appropriate class to which they belong.

When several classifications exist and/or flexibility is required for expansion, the model shown in Figure 3.5 should be used. The 'identification of classification' identifies which classification is being described, the 'level' entity type shows the level in the hierarchy and can be used to hold validation details (for example format, length), and the 'class' entity type describes the class itself and its code at that level. The class-classified entity type is an 'intersection' entity type which is required because the relationship to be classified between class and entity type is many-to-many. An example of this is shown in Figure 3.6.

The advantage of this structure is that it allows unlimited expansion of classifications and requires only one set of activities (and programs) to maintain it and provide access to it rather than a separate set for every different classification.

Therefore, the analyst has the following options when he recognises that an attribute type is classifying an entity type:

1 Represent the classification as an attribute type accepting the limitations of fixed length, difficulty of expansion and reduced access.

2 Represent the classification as an entity type in its own right, possibly with a relationship type representing its structure if it is at more than one level.

3 Represent the classification as one of the broad categories called 'classification' and identify it by its relationship with the classification identifier.

consists of

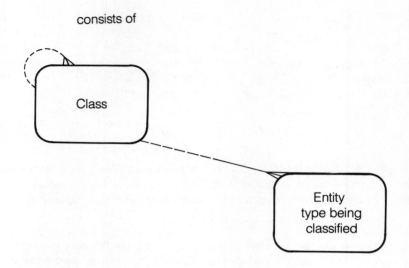

Class

Entity
type being
classified

Two classifications of a job exist: an 'occupation code' and a 'job code'

For example:

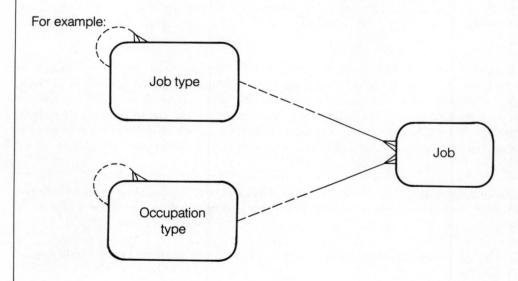

Job type

Job

Occupation
type

Figure 3.4: The model which should be used when only one or two classifications exist and there is no requirement for future expansion

84

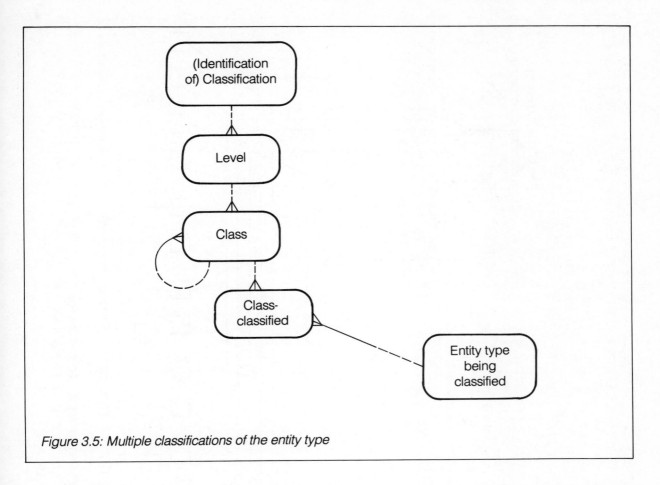

Figure 3.5: Multiple classifications of the entity type

The analyst makes his choice from his knowledge of the requirements of the system. However, in a world of changing requirements, we should always aim for the most flexible.

2.1.3 Collectives

A collective is a group of abstract or concrete objects which are collected or assembled together and given a name to describe them as a group; for example jury, department, committee. Membership of a collective varies over time and is decided by *functional* criteria. This makes a collective fundamentally different from a classification which is an inherent property of the object being classified (see Figure 3.7).

In the example shown in Figure 3.8, the total number of players available which could have been picked for either England or India is far larger than those actually picked and the choice of membership is made by selectors not because they are all male (say) or have all got blue eyes!

Collectives are more simple to represent than classifications as they are merely a form of entity type which needs to be recognised—they do not need a special structure.

2.1.4 Time and time periods

If we think of the 'entity model' as a static picture of the changing world over time, it should be apparent that the time periods over which data is kept have major significance in entity analysis. Each month, day, week and so on, expressed in the form of the calendar, for example 21 June 1981 (day) or March 1950 (month) or 1920 (year), is itself an entity type and we can classify the type of time periods by saying week, day, month and so on. In fact, time is the 'third dimension' of our model and is of such fundamental importance that without it the model is likely to be invalid. Our model must hold for all time.

The extent to which time plays a part in the model depends very much on the use to which the 'historical' data will be put. There are three fundamental ways in which time is incorporated as follows:

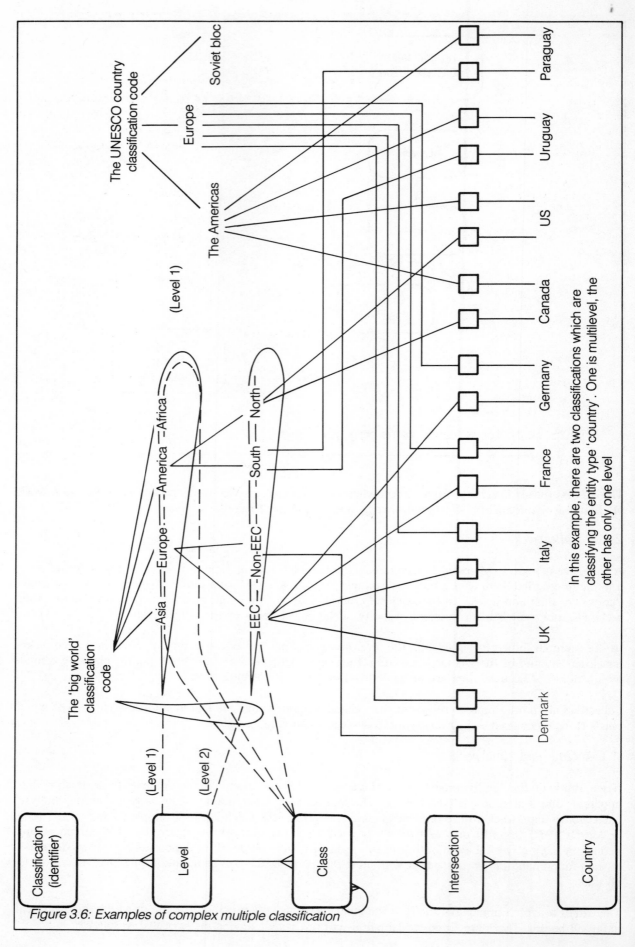

Figure 3.6: Examples of complex multiple classification

In this example, there are two classifications which are classifying the entity type 'country'. One is multilevel, the other has only one level

86

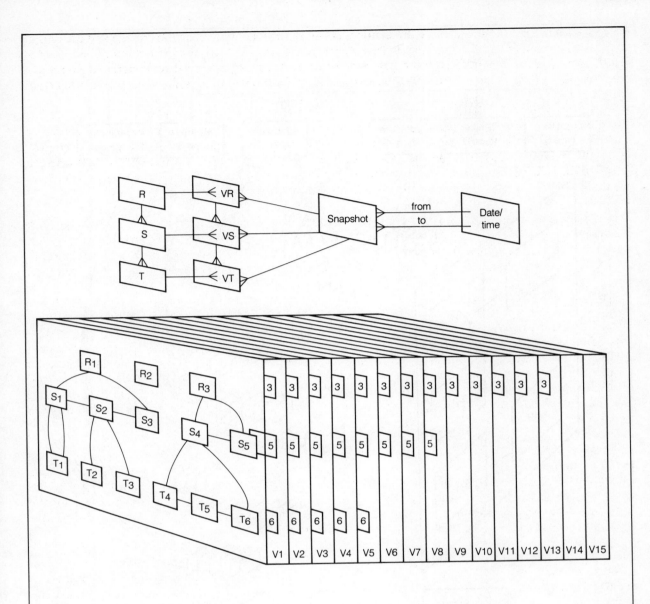

The individual occurrences of things, ie 'entities' or 'records', move through time in a number of 'time slices' or snapshots (V1 ---- V15 in our example). Each time a change is made, the occurrences are moved to a new snapshot representing the changes made. Over time, records may appear and disappear, be related to others and then not related. In this example we have R_1 related to S_1, S_2 and S_3, but in a previous version this may not have been the case.

R, S and T as entity types remain a constant feature as they model the complete picture, but 'behind' these we find the snapshots of each entity type, the snapshot to which these relate and the date and time from and to which the snapshot was valid.

Figure 3.17: The 'ultimate' or complete historical model using snapshots of the data

97

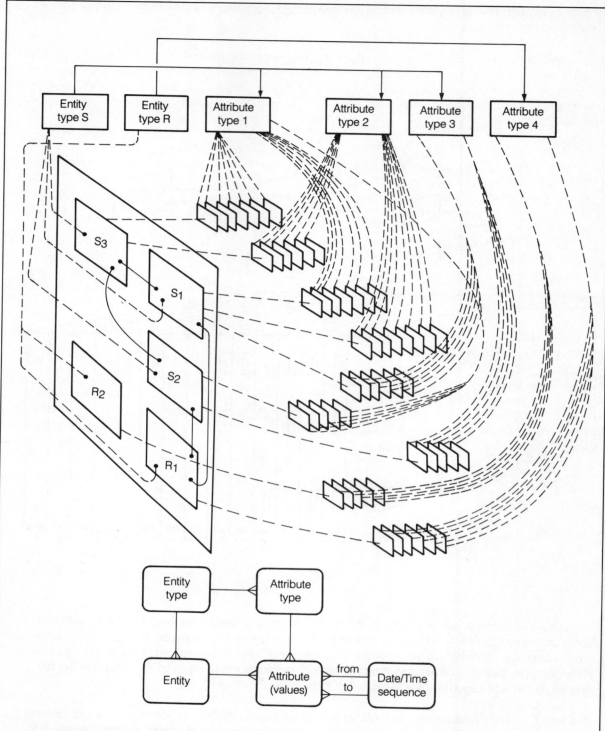

Figure 3.18: Selective snapshots on attribute value change

Views are allowed from the current back through the past to previous attributes. Each is time-stamped and identified by 'type' (for example sex, date of birth and so on). Recovery is achieved using sequence, as before, but snapshots are also possible for previous dates, though only for data which changed. The advantage is that considerably less storage is required.

not new to most people. It is a table of value combinations and actions to be performed when any of those combinations is encountered.

We can obtain simple tables with yes/no condition groups, but we are only interested in what is called a 'modified extended entry' table where a 'condition' can have more than two values (the attribute types on which the decision or action will be based have more than two values). We are going to modify the extended entry table further to produce an attribute value as a result, *not* an action. This is best shown using an example.

The problem: we have been told to calculate the delivery charges for a 'delivery' of goods (parcel). There can be two methods of delivery: air or surface. If the destination is between 10 and 20 miles and the parcel is light (under two ounces) and it is sent express surface, the rate is 15p per ounce. We can express this in tabular form, with our condition or attribute values across the top and the attribute value *dependent* on them to the left.

What we have produced is a form of decision table (see Figure 3.19) but with values in the columns and an attribute value as a result, *not an action*. In conventional decision tables the action might have read 'Multiply total weight of parcel (in ounces) by 30p'. In our version we will have the same action every time—'Multiply total weight of parcel by charging rate'—but the table will give us the charging rate. Let us continue to fill the table up.

If the method of the delivery is surface and the destination of the delivery is under 10 miles, the parcel is always sent express, whatever the weight. The charge is 20p per ounce.

We have introduced two interesting extra concepts here—the idea of an error condition and the concept of indifference—and have added them to the table. What the table now says is, if the method of delivery is surface, the mileage is under 10 miles and the service used is 'normal', *whatever the weight*, there has been *an error*. However, if the service was express, the method of delivery was surface, the destination was under 10 miles, *whatever the weight*, the charge is 20p per ounce.

Charging rate	Method of delivery	Destination of delivery	Weight of parcel (delivery)	Service used for delivery
15p/oz	Surface	10 to 20	Under 2ozs	Express
20p/oz	Surface	Under 10	–	Express
Error	Surface	Under 10	–	Normal
40p/lb	Air	Over 500 miles	Over 2lbs	N/A

Figure 3.19: Decision table for calculating delivery charges

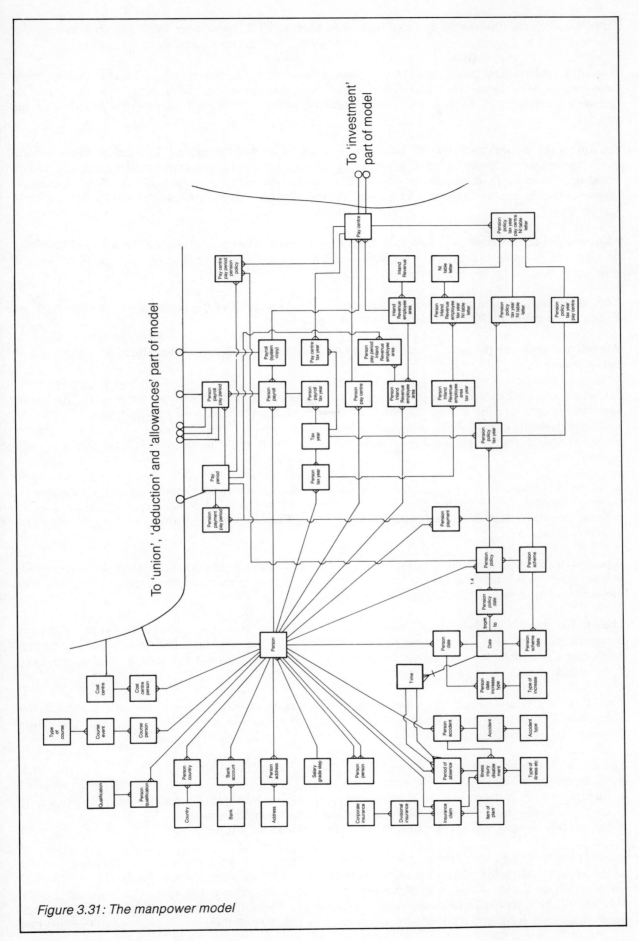

Figure 3.31: The manpower model

To 'investment' part of model

To 'union', 'deduction' and 'allowances' part of model

111

Thus, an advanced analysis course may have been held on 13-22 September 1982 and another on 1-10 January 1983 and so on. (Attribute types—date started, date finished, number of delegates.)

A person could attend more than one of these courses and the courses could be attended by more than one person, hence the intersection entity type 'course-person' with such attribute types as 'person's assessment of course event' and 'event organiser's assessment of person's performance on course'.

For a moment we will go to the left hand corner at the bottom of the model. An accident could happen in the works and be classified according to type. A person could be involved in the accident and an accident could involve more than one person, hence the intersection entity type 'person's accident'. (Attribute types—role of person in accident, offender/not offender, fatality indicator, witness or involved in indicator and so on.)

As a result of the accident, a person may suffer one or more illnesses or disabilities which were classified by type. For example, a type might be 'permanent limp' for disability or 'loss of limb' or other medical condition—just as we have in the hospital example.

Each illness may cause a number of periods of absence. As a result of the illness, the person may put in an insurance claim under the divisional insurance policy.

We will now examine the difficult side involving pensions and payroll, which introduces the complexity of *time periods*.

For all payroll and pensions models the figures are measured over different time spans according to the government body or area you are in. Thus we have the following time period entity types:
- Tax year (time period 5 April to 4 April of each year)
- Pay period (a time over which a person was paid which could be one week, four weeks or one month).

A person accumulates tax paid figures over a tax year, during which time more than one person can be accumulating tax, hence the intersection entity type person-tax year. (Attribute types—total tax paid in tax year by person, taxable income of person in tax year.) These details are sent to the Inland Revenue (IR) at year end.

A person can move payrolls within a tax year and, therefore, can accumulate tax in more than one payroll in a tax year. Thus, there is a need for an intersection entity type 'person-tax year-payroll' which describes the person's tax details in the tax year in the payroll.

The IR has an 'IR employer area' (which is its grouping of employers into areas). When a person moves IR employer area (for example Salford to London) he has what is called 'taxable income in this employment', 'taxable pay in previous employment' and 'tax paid in previous employment' which have to be carried over.

Thus there are intersection entity types *person's* membership of *IR employment area*, the tax details he accumulated in the IR's employment area in the *tax year* and the tax details he accumulated in the employment area in the *pay period*.

The following can be seen from this example:
- All intersection entity types are abstract concepts
- Intersection entity types can be formed from other intersection entity types, for example (person-IR employee area—tax year) from (tax year) and (person-IR employee area)
- Intersection entity types can be formed using time period entity types.

Analysts must recognise the existence of this important category of entity types because they are essential to the accuracy of their findings. Intersection entity types have another property however, which makes them important during *design*. It is a characteristic of all intersection entity types that they are usually *high volume*. This should be obvious, as their volumes are a multiple of the volumes of the entity types from which they were formed. Using the example in Figure 3.29, if there were 200 people, there will be *at least* 200 job histories. If five or six changes of job are recorded, then there will be some 1000 to 1200 job histories.

Efficient processing during systems design is very often dependent on optimising the database design to process high volume entity types. Thus, if the database designer can concentrate on improving access to intersection entity types and the systems designer can concentrate on improving their processing, the system is likely to be more efficient. Furthermore, if the designers know *what* to concentrate on, less effort is required on less critical entity types.

2.2.2 *Fundamental entity types*

Fundamental entity types exist in their own right and do not owe their existence to any others.

There are some fundamental entity types which appear time and time again in business models and can therefore be looked on as more 'fundamental' than others. They are as follows:
- Business (customer, suppliers, clients etc)
- Person
- Geographical locations
  —country
  —address
  —town etc
- Organisation (of the business)
- Time periods
  —date
  —year
  —week etc.

Fundamental entity types are usually characterised by the following important properties that have a dramatic effect during design:
- Low volume
- Not volatile (that is, require minimal updating).

Because they are low volume, systems performance and database design will not be critical, so the designers can concentrate less on these entity types than on the intersection entity types.

They are also very suitable candidates for the type of on-line processing which groups all activities under the following categories:
- Insert
- Amend
- Delete (or archive)
- Print (one)
- List (according to certain criteria (attribute values)).

Intersection entity types cannot easily be handled in this way because of their dependence on other entity types for their existence. A number of cross checks, to ensure that the 'owners' exist and that consistency is maintained, are usually inherent to their creation and maintenance.

2.2.3 *Summary*

The classification of fundamental/intersection entity types has importance both in analysis (as the analyst must recognise the existence of these important groups) and in design where the properties of the two groups indicate on which areas of the model the designer should concentrate and how the entity types might be processed.

2.3 Basic or derived

An essential classification which must be recognised by the analyst is that of the basic or derived entity type. A basic entity type has not been created using the attribute values from other entity types, but a derived entity type has.

Events	Attribute type	Attribute values	Mutually exclusive group
1 Patient referred to hospital	Patient's hospital status	Referred	Referred patients
Patient discharged from hospital		Discharged	Discharged patients
Patient admitted to hospital		Admitted	Admitted patients
2 Appointment attended by patient	Appointment status	Kept	Appointments kept
Appointment not attended by patient		Broken	Appointments broken
Appointment cancelled		Cancelled	Appointments cancelled
Appointment booked		Booked	Appointments booked

Figure 3.40: Combining mutually exclusive groups of entities

Therefore where we need to keep a record of events, we must identify each set of mutually exclusive groups of events and allocate an attribute type to each or, if no mutually exclusive groups exist, allocate one attribute type to each event with attribute values equivalent to 'yes' (the event has happened) or 'no' (it has not). The result is a list of attribute types which represent either permanent classifications of an entity type or the events which will affect the entity type.

As can be seen in Figure 3.41, there is only one permanent classification. This is not unusual. However, it is most unusual to find many 'states' which are not changed over time. One could argue that since we use a hospital example, even the permanent classification shown could be impermanent!

In order to determine attribute types, it is important to consider *every* event which may affect the entity type and on which system functions are dependent. So, events such as 'enquiry into health of patient' may not be of interest because no subsequent functions are dependent on knowing that this has happened. However, knowledge of events such as the following is important:
- 'Birth of patient'
- 'Death of patient'
- 'Appointment made'.

This is because knowledge of their existence and recording the fact that they have happened are essential for the further processing of subsequent events. For example, you cannot cancel an appointment unless you know it has been made. Therefore, we should think of our system as an event recording system which can protect itself against corruption and is more robust.

4.4 Permanent or transient

Just as with entity types, the existence of transient attribute types is as important as permanent attribute types. The reason that 'working storage' is used in programs is often to record transient attribute types. However, there is a real danger that attribute types which are of importance to other activities will be lost because the analyst *thinks* they are transient and makes the arbitrary decision to ignore them.

Entity type	Attribute types	Event	Permanent/Impermanent
Patient	Sex indicator - male - female		Perm
	Date of referral	Referred	Imp
	Date of death	Death	Imp
	Date of birth	Born	Imp
	Marital status		
	- married	Marries	
	- divorced	Divorces	Imp
	- widowed	Widowed	
	(no history required, only current state)		
	Date of discharge	Discharge	Imp
	Date admitted	Admitted to hospital	Imp

Figure 3.41: Permanent classifications of an entity type

All attribute types must be defined, and we are only more certain about the 'life' of an attribute type after analysis is complete (at the detailed stage). If it then appears to be transient—lasting for only one (or perhaps two) activities—the decision can be made *by the designer* as to how it will be held (on a 'transaction file' or a 'work table' or in the working storage of a program).

It is not for the analyst to make decisions about the means of design. He must use his judgement to help the designer in his choice. An attribute type lasting only one activity may seem, to the designer, to be a prime candidate for working storage, but the analyst may be aware that there are long-term plans which could result in activities to make more use of the attribute type—he must explain this to the designer.

However, the analyst does not make decisions about which attribute types are 'important' and which are not. All attribute types—even if they are used in one minor activity—must be defined or the results of analysis will be incomplete and the activity analysis results meaningless.

5 Permitted values

These are allowable values used to describe an entity and which are classified using an attribute type. A synonym for a permitted value is 'attribute' and the complete range of permitted values allowed for an attribute type is known as the domain. There are two main categories: the range of permitted values and single permitted values.

It was explained earlier that a range was only a shorthand way of describing permitted values when the potential number became impossible to describe singly. Within the single permitted value category there are three important sub-categories, as follows:

1 The code.
2 The quantitative value.
3 The fixed narrative.

5.1 Codes

A code is a fixed length representation of a value. It is used when the actual values have a large number of characters or are not of fixed length. The main types are as follows:

- Alpha or numeric or alphanumeric code
- Self-checking code
- Classification code
- Mnemonic code.

5.1.1 *Alpha or numeric or mixed*

An alphanumeric non-significant code is an alphabetic or numeric or mixed value code, of fixed length, which is assigned to a data value. It has no significance and is arbitrarily assigned to the permitted meanings which are identified. This type of code is unsuitable for classifications as it does not provide the ability to represent the structure of the classification. It can be used for all *one*-level classifications.

In general a numeric code is more reliable than an alphabetic code if no significance is intended. There are more errors in communicating alphabetic codes by telephone—hence the common use of a phonetic alphabet. If alphanumeric codes are considered, they should be controlled rather than using random alphanumeric codes. Thus, each character should be *either* a number *or* a letter, not both. For example, A9999 or AA99A.

5.1.2 *Self-checking codes*

It is possible to append an additional character to a code which checks the consistency or validity of it when it is recorded and transferred from one point to another. The character, commonly called a *check character*, is derived by using some mathematical technique involving the characters in the base code.

5.1.3 *Classification codes*

One of the problems with coding classifications is allowing enough room for expansion. If each level in the classification is defined separately and given a fixed format, the format must be such that it is sufficiently 'flexible' to allow expansion (see Figure 3.42).

Because we have this 'within, within, within' structure, the result of inadequate planning for expansion can cause more problems than an ordinary one-level classification.

If we have a one-level classification and we have 10 values already, the format of 99 is likely to be more than adequate for expansion. If we have between 50 and 60 values and we choose 999, again we have adequate room. However, by 'playing safe' in a classification of more than one level, we can make the resulting code enormous.

The Dewey decimal system is used primarily for indexing libraries or classifying written correspondence by subject matter. Figure 3.43 is a representative example.

Level 1	Level 2	Level 3
9 9	9 9	9 9 9

Level 1 allows 100 top-level classifications
Level 2 allows 100 values within a level 1 value
Level 3 allows 1000 values within a level 2 value

Figure 3.42: Allowing for expansion in coding

Model version	Strategic	Overview	Detailed
401 Version number	✓	✓	✓
402 Date from	✓	✓	✓
403 Date to	✓	✓	✓
404 Agreed/under discussion/rejected	✓	✓	✓
405 Users agreeing/rejecting	✓	✓	✓
406 Abbreviated name	✓	✓	✓
407 Advantages	✓	✓	✓
408 Disadvantages	✓	✓	✓
409 Proposed by (users)	✓	✓	✓
413 Responsibility			
414 Analyst responsible/allowed to look	✓	✓	✓
415 Type of access allowed	✓	✓	✓
416 Chief/deputy	✓	✓	✓
417 Date last accessed	✓	✓	✓
418 Descriptive name	✓	✓	✓
419 Type of model Fuzzy	✓	✓	✓
Overview			
Detailed			

Figure 4.4: Model versions

Permitted values and ranges	Strategic	Overview	Detailed
501 Permitted values			
502 Value (code or other)			✓
503 Value name			✓
504 Value meaning/definition			✓
505 Value abbreviated name			✓
506 Start date			✓
507 End date			✓
508 Not known value? (Y/N)			✓
509 Null value? (Y/N)			✓
510 Initial or default value? (Y/N)			✓
511 Permitted ranges			
512 Maximum value			✓
513 Minimum value			✓
514 Start date			✓
515 End date			✓

Figure 4.5: Permitted values and ranges

Design and design mapping	Strategic	Overview	Detailed
Data item			
301 Name of data item			✓
302 Descriptive name			✓
303 Format			✓
304 Codes/ranges			
304 Code/range			✓
305 Responsibility			
306 Designer			✓
307 Type of access			✓
308 Date last accessed			✓
309 Chief/deputy			✓
Record type			
601 Name		✓	✓
602 Descriptive name		✓	✓
603 Responsibility			
604 Designer		✓	✓
605 Type of access		✓	✓
606 Date last accessed		✓	✓
607 Chief/deputy		✓	✓
File type			
701 Name	✓	✓	✓
702 Descriptive name	✓	✓	✓
703 Responsibility			
704 Designer	✓	✓	✓
705 Type of access	✓	✓	✓
706 Date last accessed	✓	✓	✓
707 Chief/deputy	✓	✓	✓
710 Record-file usage			
710 Usage		✓	✓
721 Record partitioning			
722 Partitioning criteria		✓	✓
723 Maximum records for that partition		✓	✓
724 File/record occurrences			
725 Number of records of that type		✓	✓
726 Date to which figures apply		✓	✓
711 File implementations			
712 Type of implementation		✓	✓
713 Implementation name		✓	✓
714 File implementation name		✓	✓
715 Descriptive name		✓	✓
716 File mapping			
717 File mapping name			✓
718 Physical file identifier			✓
719 Date from			✓
720 Date to			✓

Figure 4.6a: Design and design mapping

	Strategic	Overview	Detailed
Set/link			
801 Name		✓	✓
802 Descriptive name		✓	✓
803 Ends			
803 End name		✓	✓
804 Responsibility			
805 Designer		✓	✓
806 Type of access		✓	✓
807 Date last accessed		✓	✓
808 Chief/deputy		✓	✓
Implementation			
901 Name	✓	✓	✓
902 Full descriptive name	✓	✓	✓
903 Responsibility			
904 Designer	✓	✓	✓
905 Type of access allowed	✓	✓	✓
906 Date last accessed	✓	✓	✓
907 Chief/deputy	✓	✓	✓
System			
1001 Usage	✓	✓	✓
1002 Proposed/current	✓	✓	✓
1003 Name	✓	✓	✓
1004 Short name	✓	✓	✓
1005 Description	✓	✓	✓
1006 Responsibility			
1007 Designer	✓	✓	✓
1008 Type of access allowed	✓	✓	✓
1009 Date last accessed	✓	✓	✓
1010 Chief/deputy	✓	✓	✓
Mapping of analysis to design concepts			
1101 Attribute mapping			
1102 Most reliable source			✓
1103 Code mapping			
1104 Mapping match			✓
1105 Entity mapping			
1106 Most reliable source		✓	✓
1107 Relationship type mapping			
1108 Most reliable source		✓	✓
1109 Entity group mapping			
1110 Mapping	✓		
1111 Record partitioning/entity type partitioning mapping			
1112 Most reliable source		✓	✓
1113 Entity occurrence mapping			
1114 Mapping		✓	✓

Figure 4.6b: Design and design mapping (cont)

The deliverables have been organised around the four building blocks of entity analysis, which will now be examined, as follows:

1 Facts required about entity types.
2 Facts required about relationship types.
3 Facts required about attribute types.
4 Facts required about permitted values.

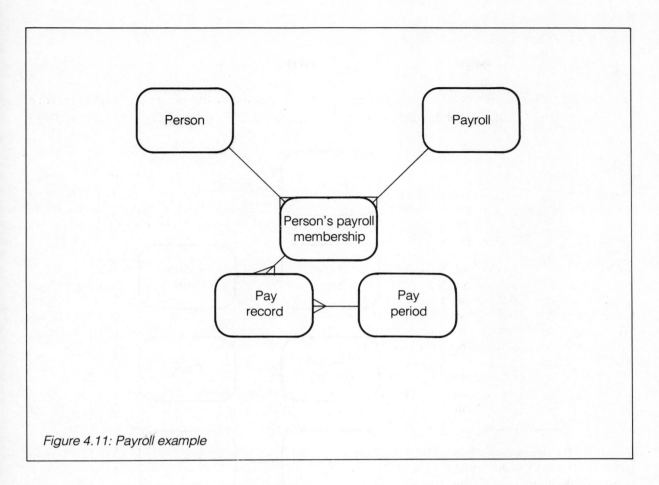

Figure 4.11: Payroll example

between the person's payroll membership and the pay period. The entity model of this example is shown in Figure 4.11.

This example shows adequately the importance of the time entity type (in this case pay period) to the definition of the entity types. Let us now consider a more complex example to explore these possibilities further.

Example 2—order entry
In this example we are dealing with the problem of orders and deliveries. Let us assume that we start with the following well understood foundation entity types:

- Order—a command or request from one business to another to supply goods or services
- Product type—the different types of products the business makes (generalised abstract entity type of the concrete entity type product, that is, the actual visible products of the business)
- Business—an abstract entity type describing a firm organisation or part of that organisation
- Vehicle—a concrete entity type describing a car, lorry or other vehicle
- Location address—a physical place which can be described by its address (concrete)
- Date—day, month and year
- Time—hour of the day in hours and minutes.

Firstly we look at the relationship of order to product type. It is many-to-many (many product types can be on an order and, similarly, a product type can have been ordered many times). Therefore, there is an intersection entity type known to the business as an 'order item'. We may define this as 'the request for *one product type on one order*'.

Let us assume that as a result of the order each order item is broken down with a series of 'planned deliveries'. How do we define 'planned deliveries'? We must use the concepts already available, so we would say 'the planned delivery of one *product type* on *one order* on *one date*' where the planned delivery is understood (if it was not, we would define this too; for example, planned by whom?). The model is shown in Figure 4.12.

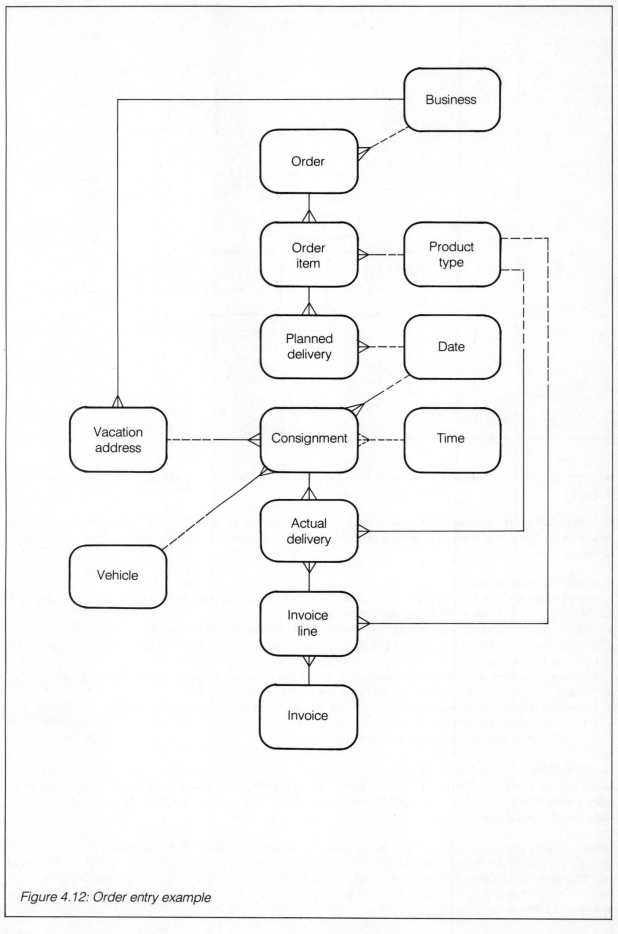

Figure 4.12: Order entry example

Later the system will produce an 'actual delivery' which is part of a 'consignment'. Actual delivery has the synonym 'goods received note'. Again, we must use our base entity types to define these new concepts as follows:

1 *Consignment:* the actual delivery on one *date* by one *vehicle* to one *location address* of a consignment of goods (which may be of different types).

2 *Actual delivery (goods received note):* the actual delivery on one *date* by one *vehicle* to one *location address* of one *product type* from one *order*. Note that the omission of only one entity type completely alters the definition. For example, the removal of location address in the consignment definition would then imply that the delivery was to a series of addresses and the 'consignment' was probably describing the load of the lorry. We can tighten up these definitions further by adding the words 'at one time'. It is then clear that we are actually describing a 'point event'.

If we then group the actual deliveries we have made so that they are grouped according to the business they were made to and charge the business on this basis, we have created an invoice which has lines for each product and we can base our definition of invoice on this basis.

3 *Invoice:* a demand for payment from one business to another for goods received.

4 *Invoice line:* a demand for payment from one business to another for a *type of product* delivered.

It should be clear from this example that if we get the original definition of our fundamental entity types wrong, the rest of the definitions will be wrong and ambiguous. For example, at the moment the definition of 'business' is too loose as it does not define precisely what we mean and it could lead to confusion.

2.4.5 *Common errors*

The most common errors which arise in producing a definition are as follows:

1 *Ambiguity:* this occurs when the term has not been defined precisely enough. Conflict arises when it is not clear whether a particular entity comes within the definition or not. For example, the long dispute between the US and England, called the Alabama Case, turned on the meaning of the expression 'to equip a ship of war'. International law allowed the building and selling of 'ships of war', provided that they were not sent out fully equipped for fighting. The dispute arose from the differences of opinion as to what 'equip' meant.

2 *Homonyms:* where one word serves many purposes; for example 'church'. This could mean a building or the body of people representing a religion (the Church of England).

3 *Difficulty in deriving a general definition:* for example, the term 'house' can be used so specifically that it may be difficult to derive a meaning general enough to cover all types of house. The danger is that the definition may exclude certain types of house which you want to include (dwelling house (people), cow house, counting-house and so on).

4 *Misuse of a term:* using a term in the wrong sense.

5 *Assumption:* assuming that a term is clear when it is not. For example, the term order. Many people assume that this is self explanatory, but does it mean sales order or purchase order? Does it include contracts or not?

2.4.6 *Summary*

The precise and unambiguous definition of entity types is essential to the correct functioning of a system, whether it is existing or newly designed. Without precise definition the system is likely to fail because no common language exists to ensure that it is operated as intended. To build up this definition we must use concrete or abstract entity types which are well understood, precisely defined and describe commonly understood concepts. The analyst has a clear role to ensure that the definitions produced for entity types are using a common base language which is understood by every person involved in making the system work.

2.5 Entity subtypes (13)

2.5.1 *Definition*

Entity subtypes are mutually exclusive groups of entities within the one entity type. For example, if the entity type is 'person', we may have one classification of male and female subtypes. Alternatively, another classification may be the subtypes 'married' or 'not married'. If we think of all the possible ways we may want to classify our total population of entities within the type, we can see that there will be many likely ways they can be divided.

For example, our entity type 'person' may have the following classifications and, hence, subtypes:

Classification	Subtypes
Sex	Male
	Female
Marital status	Married
	Single
	Divorced
	Widowed
Age classification	Child
	Adult
	Pensioner

Within each grouping chosen, however, an entity can belong to *ONE* subtype only. For example, a person is either male or female, either married *or* single *or* divorced *or* widowed, and either a child *or* an adult *or* a pensioner.

As more and more classifications are applied, we effectively divide our total population into smaller and smaller groups which are defined by the subtypes they belong to (see Figure 4.13). Ultimately, if we continue to apply more and more classifications, we will probably have a population of one per group of subtypes.

We can also show this effect pictorially, using a Venn diagram (see Figure 4.14) in which our classifications are sex (subtypes: 'male' and 'female') and employee status (subtypes: 'nurses', 'doctors', 'others').

There are two types of entity subtype as follows:

1 *Permanent subtypes:* these are permanent states, conditions or modes of existence, which are fixed over time and are event-independent. Consider these examples: an entity type 'tree' might have the subtypes 'hardwood' or 'softwood', 'deciduous' or 'evergreen' and so on. These states will never change in a tree's life and are therefore permanent. An entity type 'automobile' might be a bus, car or lorry. A 'building' might be a hospital, clinic or operating theatre.

2 *Impermanent subtypes:* these describe modes of existence which are not fixed over time and which are entirely event-dependent. For example a 'person' can be an employee or not an employee, married or not married, a child, an adult or a retired adult. An example is shown in Figure 4.15.

Each property which classifies the population into subtypes is represented by an attribute type, and each mutually exclusive group of entities is described by an attribute value. For example:
- Property = Sex
- Attribute type = Sex
- Attribute values = Male, Female.

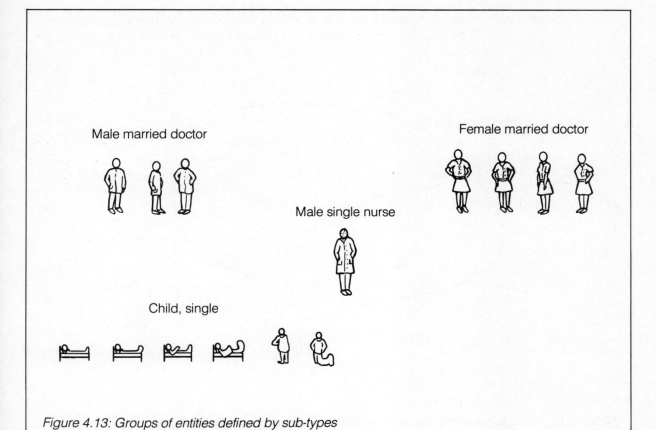

Male married doctor

Female married doctor

Male single nurse

Child, single

Figure 4.13: Groups of entities defined by sub-types

Employees

Men

Women

Nurses

Doctors

Men

Women

Others

Figure 4.14: Venn diagrams used to explain independent subtype groups

153

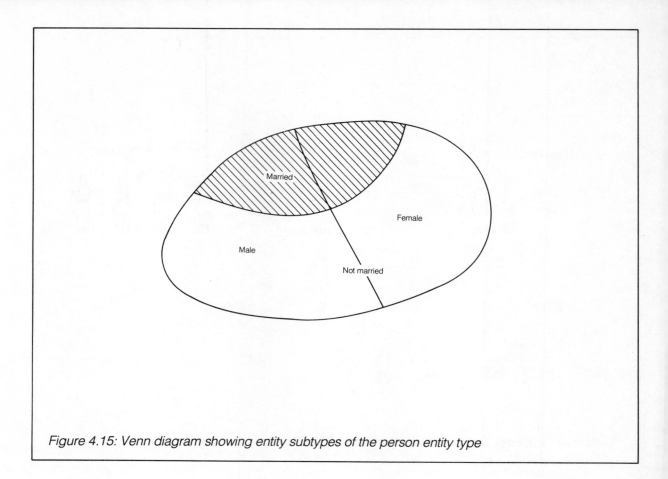

Figure 4.15: Venn diagram showing entity subtypes of the person entity type

Only 'pure' properties must be used, they must not be combined to produce 'mixed' classifications. For example the sex/marital status code:
- Male married
- Female married
- Male single
- Female single.

The attribute types which result may be event recording or inherent property recording, more details of which were given in Chapter 3.

2.5.2 *Purposes*

1 *Database design:* where subtypes exist there is always a split in population. In the example of Figure 4.16a, for example, there may be only 1000 banks but 50 000 residents. Wherever subtypes have their own attributes, space (sometimes considerable space) can be wasted by having one record type, especially where there is little shared data or where extra pointers/indexes are required for a low volume subtype (which are not applicable for the high volume remainder). This is shown in Figure 4.16b.

A database designer, using details of entity subtype volumes and attribute type and relationship type applicability, may split the entity type into more than one record type to save space (see Figure 4.16c).

Alternatively, he may use variable length records or 'compressed' records.

Only permanent subtypes should be used when splitting entity types to create record types. This is to avoid the problem of 'migrating populations', that is records which have to move across record types on the change of status.

154

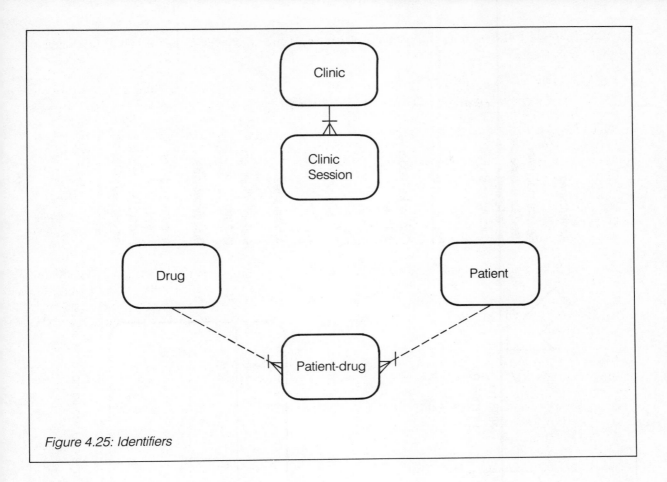

Figure 4.25: Identifiers

2.6.2 Diagrammatic representation

Where an entity type is identified (in part or in full) by its relationship with another entity type, this is represented on the model by a stroke across the relationship type nearest the entity type identified by it.

In Figure 4.25 an example is shown where the entity type 'patient-drug' is identified by its relationship with both the patient and the drug.

Where a mixture of attribute types and relationship types is used to identify an entity type, the stroke is still placed on the model, as in Figure 4.25 where the clinic session was identified by its relationship with the clinic but *also* the attribute type session number which was unique within a clinic number. Note that the symbol is actually representing a *mandatory non-transferable* relationship type.

Where an entity type is identified by attribute types no symbol is used on the model, but the identifying attributes can be written on the model, by the entity type or inside the box itself (see Figure 4.26). The advantage of recording by the entity type (as a list) is that, during access path analysis, the identifier can be indicated directly by pointing to it.

2.6.3 Purposes

2.6.3.1 Database and file design

The primary reason why identifiers are required is to enable the designer to select the attribute type(s) which will be the key of the records he designs. Those identifiers not chosen as the primary key may have to be 'secondary indexes' to the record type if access is also required by them (see Figure 4.27).

Whenever a record must be *accessed directly* (one record is found directly using a key value), a key must be present. If only attribute types are used to identify the entity type the choice is simple. However, if relationship types are also used, the designer has to choose which identifiers to use, as the 'owning' entity types may have more than one.

163

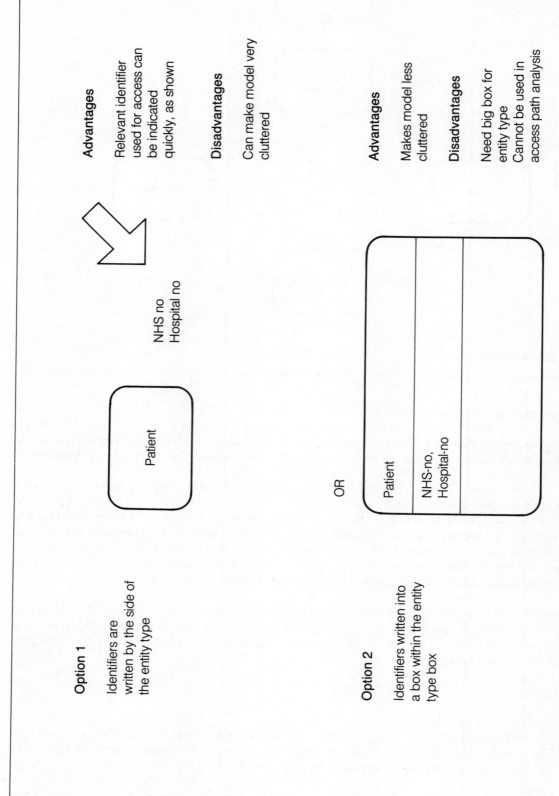

Option 1

Identifiers are written by the side of the entity type

NHS no
Hospital no

Advantages

Relevant identifier used for access can be indicated quickly, as shown

Disadvantages

Can make model very cluttered

OR

Option 2

Identifiers written into a box within the entity type box

Patient

NHS-no,
Hospital-no

Advantages

Makes model less cluttered

Disadvantages

Need big box for entity type
Cannot be used in access path analysis

(The identifier symbols are only applicable at the detailed analysis stage and should not normally be shown to users, where the extra complexity may only confuse)

Figure 4.26: Identification by attributes – symbolic representation

164

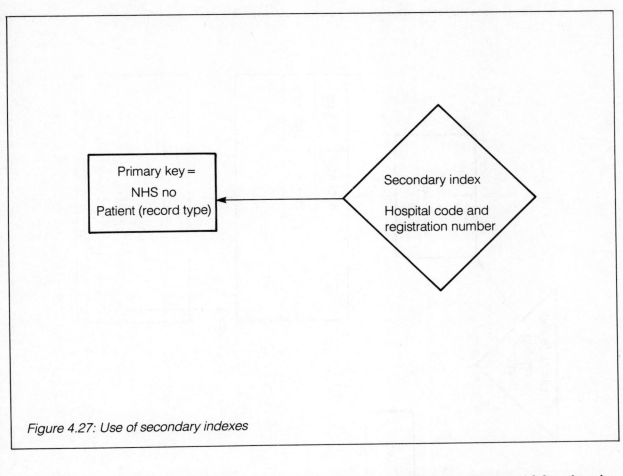

Figure 4.27: Use of secondary indexes

In Figure 4.28 an example is given where, because the illness entity type had to be accessed directly, a key had to be found. In analysis terms it was identified by its relationship to patient, illness type and the dates. The date and illness type only had one identifier, so the choice was easy—these identifiers were used as part of the key of the illness record. The patient had two identifiers, so a choice had to be made based on the *activity requirements*. Thus, activity analysis plays an important part at this stage.

Keys can only be formed using this method of 'embedding' *if the relationship type is part of the identifier*. If the stroke does not exist on the model, then embedding owner keys *is not permitted* and a key/identifier will have to be invented. Guidelines on this are given later. These rules are as true for CODASYL-based DBMSs as they are for relational or 'part-network' DBMSs such as TOTAL and IMAGE.

The terms used in analysis of mandatory

contingent

and fully optional

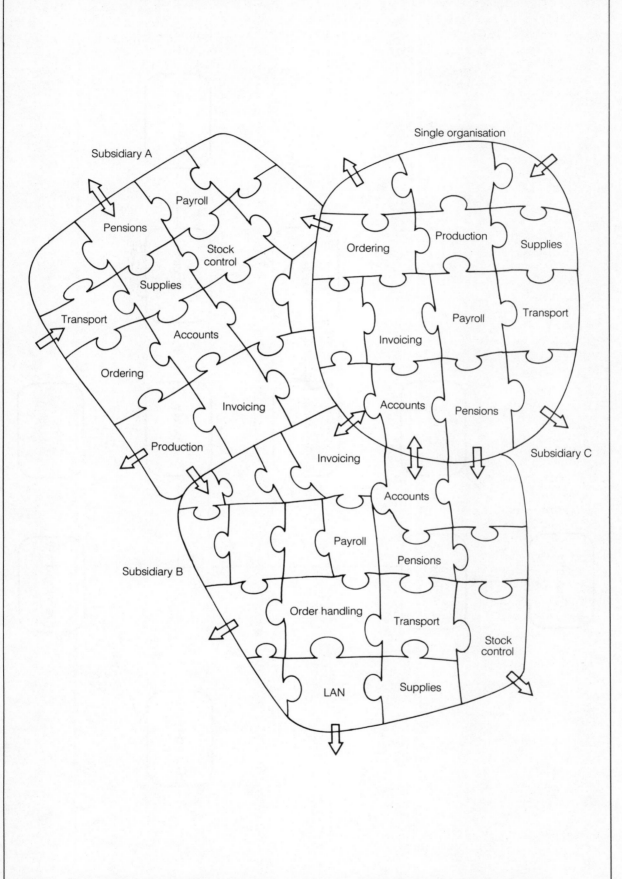

Figure 4.33: Multiple organisation or interaction with other organisations (the systems 'jigsaw')

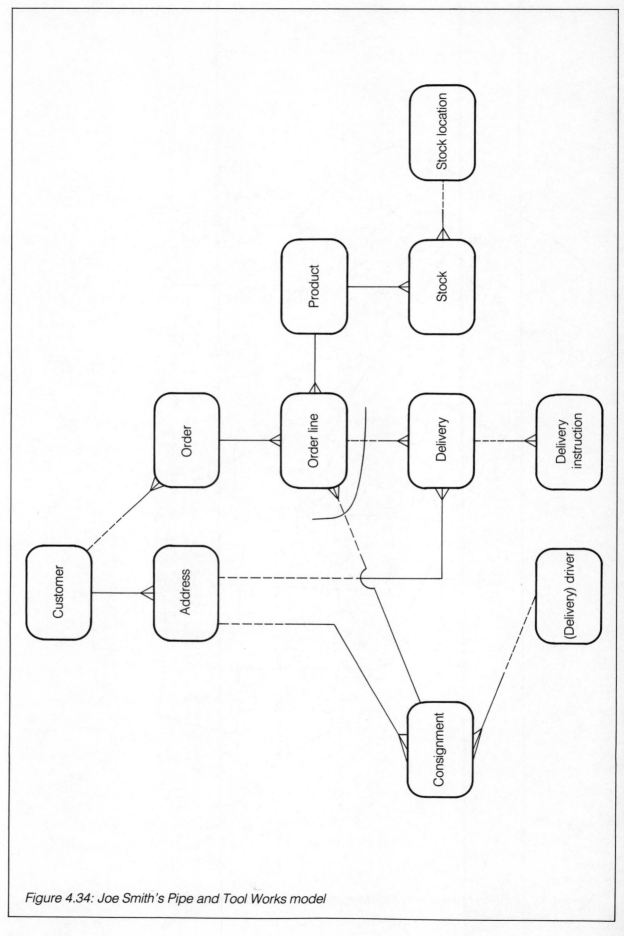

Figure 4.34: Joe Smith's Pipe and Tool Works model

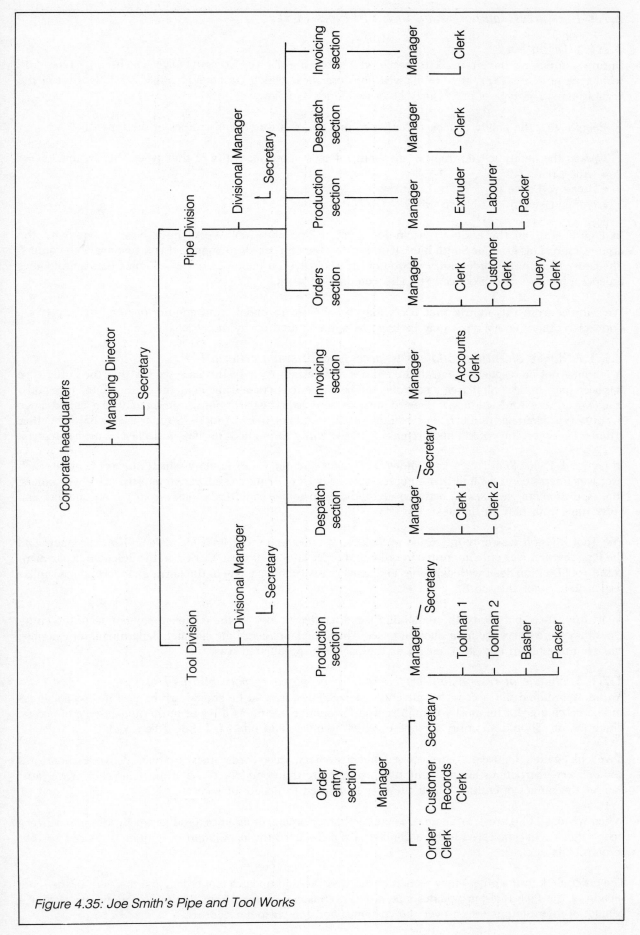

Figure 4.35: Joe Smith's Pipe and Tool Works

'limited usage' and 'private' and are rough categorisations to describe the level of interest in these entity types.

2.7.2.2 *Purposes*

1 *Package selection/'standard systems':* it should be clear from the figure that the Tool Division has a different system when delivering goods to that of the Pipe Division. The Tool Division splits its orders into deliveries, which are gradually fulfilled from a stock which is replenished by the production department which makes very large batches of tools, not to order, but on the basis of general demand. The Pipe Division makes to order and has no stock. When it has manufactured all of a customer's order it despatches one consignment with the option of grouping order lines if the whole order is ready at once. Furthermore, the despatch department of the Tool Division adds delivery instructions to each delivery note—the Pipe Division does not. However, the Pipe Division employs its own drivers who may be allocated to deliver a consignment.

In this case it should be clear that a 'standard system' approach for 'ordering' in Joe Smith's company is totally inappropriate. The business of the two subsidiaries is so different that a 'standard system' developed for one would not fit for the other and one developed to cover both would be highly complex to operate.

The reasons why companies develop 'standard systems' or buy packages are as follows:
- To save development effort
- To impose standard procedures on the organisations or subsidiaries to achieve uniformity; for example, standard accounting procedures, payroll calculations or pay dates.

The major reason why this approach often fails is that it imposes a standard procedure on an area which does not use this system. Thus, this simple chart should show, at a glance, whether 'standard systems' are appropriate.

2 *Effort pay back:* there is more benefit to be derived from producing a system which has many users than one which has very few users. Therefore, it follows that there is more benefit to be derived from supporting 'corporate' and 'limited usage' entity types than in supporting 'private' entity types. The effort expended should be in direct proportion to the number of users who will benefit.

2.7.2.3 *Hints and guidelines*

There are dangers with placing too much emphasis on applicability which must be recognised and allowed for during analysis, as follows:
- If there is reorganisation, the chart becomes obsolete
- There is a danger that entity types at private and limited usage level may be corporate, but other users have not recognised the fact. Presentation of the full model may help to remedy this.

2.7.3 *Partitioning (30)*

2.7.3.1 *Definition*

The entity types accessed by jobs within the organisation were shown in Figure 4.42, together with the partitioning which occurred. From this we can derive the organisational unit at which partitioning (if any) occurs. If no partitioning occurs, the level of applicability applies. Thus, partitioning describes: the organisational unit at which the population of an entity type permanently divides (31); and what defines the partitioning made (32).

2.7.3.2 *Diagrammatic representation*

Figure 4.43 shows the partitioning of Joe Smith's works. All corporate entity types (those with universal applicability) are shown at the 'corporate' level. Only those where 'all' entities of the entity type were of interest are shown and, in our case, this reduces the original five to two—'customer' and 'customer address'. This implies that all entities of these types are of interest to all the organisation units at the next lowest level.

The 'order' entity type has applicability to the Managing Director where *all* orders are needed, but the population is *split* between Pipe and Tool Divisions. The 'order line' and 'product' entity types have completely split populations and, as we have already seen, 'stock' and 'stock location' are unique to the

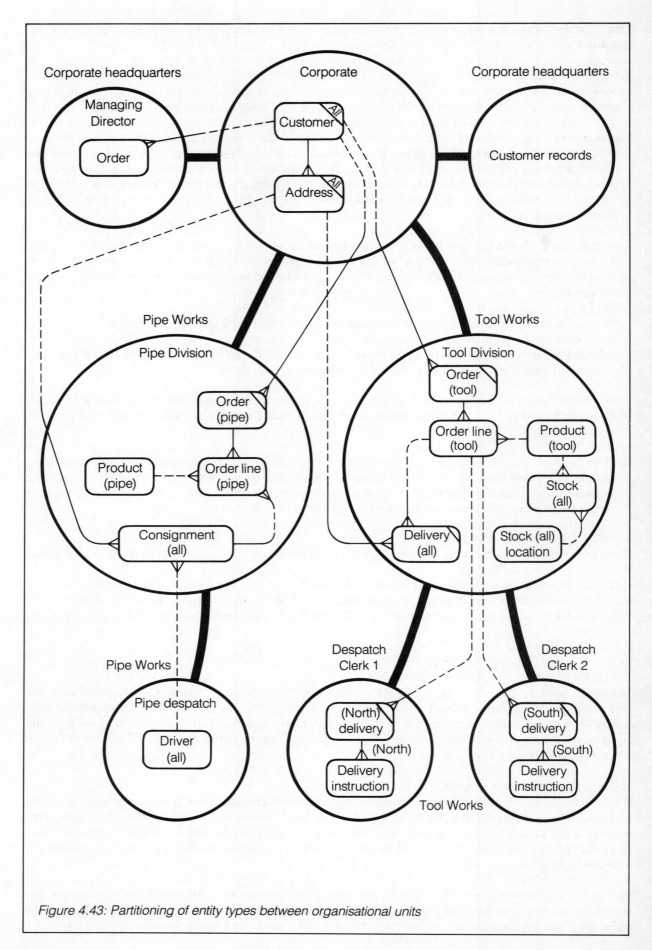

Figure 4.43: Partitioning of entity types between organisational units

Tool Division, whereas 'consignment' is unique to the Pipe Division. All 'deliveries' are required at Tool Division level, but at the despatch level the populations are split between 'north' and 'south'. Delivery instructions are also split at this level, but have no divisional relevance. Pipe despatch uses all 'drivers'. The customer records section has no entity types but maintains the corporate entity types of 'customer' and 'customer address'.

2.7.3.3 *Purposes*

Location plays an important part in the hardware planner's job. Once 'organisation' divisions have been identified, as shown in Figure 4.43, we can then use the *locations* of each organisational unit to determine the configuration required. Let us assume that Joe Smith himself and his customer records section resided at 'Corporate Headquarters', physically separate from the Pipe and Tool Works—effectively there are three locations.

The main point of concern for the planner will be the traffic on the channels between the three locations and how it can be reduced. He uses the activity figures to determine the likely volume of traffic.

The detail given in Figure 4.43 shows that the areas of likely *required duplication of data* are the 'order' (Corporate HQ, Pipe Works, Tool Works) and, because they are corporate, 'customer' and 'customer address' (Corporate HQ, Pipe Works, Tool Works).

There is duplication at the three locations of the entities 'customer' and 'customer address'. There is *no duplication* between Pipe and Tool Works for the 'order', but there is between Corporate HQ and the Pipe Works and Corporate HQ and the Tool Works.

The hardware planner examines the response figures to assess the impact. Corporate HQ does not require up to date order data, thus 'refreshing' of the duplicated corporate order data could take place overnight.

The tool and pipe nodes do require timely customer data. Customer *queries* are higher at the three locations than updates. Thus, to minimise traffic, the customer master could be placed at Corporate HQ and updated from there with updates passed on-line to the two other locations.

To a hardware planner, the detail being collected helps him decide on the following:
- Where duplication of data is required
- Where partitioning of data is applicable
- Where data should physically reside
- The frequency of 'refreshing' between locations.

2.7.3.4 *Hints and guidelines*

All this detail is only required because a major part of the cost of hardware is channel costs, which are based primarily on usage. So the objective is to try to reduce these.

Duplication is not desirable; it creates serious problems if there is channel failure as data rapidly becomes out of date. Furthermore, duplication costs money in terms of storage and writing extra software.

It is more likely that data should be as up to date as possible, rather than of the 'delayed' timeliness variety discussed earlier. This is because, generally speaking, data has a 'knock-on' effect; for example, a customer's credit rating affects the acceptance of orders which, in turn, affects production, stocking and so on. Out of date data in the 'operations' part of a company is usually unacceptable and can lead to all sorts of problems (over-stocking, over-manufacture, wrong payments).

'Distributed data' is one of the major characteristics of a clerical system, but the disadvantage of such a system is not that it is run by people (this I regard as a major advantage because people are more flexible) but that it causes problems with data. Clerical systems *force* the distribution of data which results in massive duplication and inconsistency, an enormous waste of effort in updating, unnecessary redundancy, lack of timeliness of information and so on. As an example of this, I was once asked to help in the analysis of a system which was entirely clerically based. Although only a few departments were involved—all in the same building—they had developed 16 different forms which recorded the same entity type. In each case the form recorded *slightly* different data (an extra attribute type or the entity type's relationship with other things), no two forms were exactly the same but, in general, there was massive duplication.

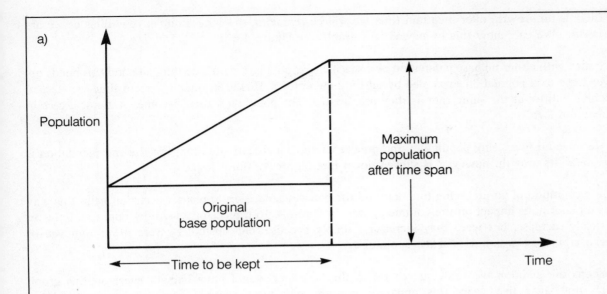

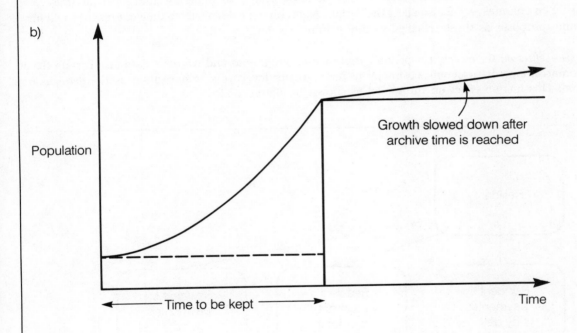

Figure 4.50: Cumulative and non-cumulative growth patterns
Figure 4.50a: No growth in new entities (non-cumulative)
Figure 4.50b: Growth in new entities (cumulative)

If there is no growth, after a certain time we will be removing the same number of entities as we are receiving. We can show this by means of a graph (see Figure 4.50a).

We start with either no base population or a specific base population on a certain date and this builds up, over time, to a population expanded by all the new entities. However, after a certain time we start to archive entities at the same rate as they are created. The population then becomes static at a certain maximum level.

If we have an increasing population and *growth* we have a similar situation, but the end population is *not static*. Its growth, however, is slowed down (see Figure 4.50b).

The recognition of an archiving function and the conscious decision to restrict occurrences in this way has an enormous impact on the volume figures. In Figure 4.46 the customer entities appeared to be on a steady increase, but were they increasing simply because 'old' customers were never removed or because business was indeed truly 'booming'?

Perhaps the addition of archiving criteria to the customer would have had an effect on this graph such that after five years this apparent growth may have slowed down. For example: event signalling end of life equals *last* order paid for; number of years after event customer details to be kept is five years.

3 *Database design:* just as volumes are important for database design, so archiving rules—because they have an impact on volumes—will also affect the design. As archiving rules affect volume figures they will have the same purposes as those specified in the 'volume' section.

4 *Analysis—effect on the model:* it is possible that as time progresses and we have data at a certain 'level' of summarisation, the user will be happy to have greater levels of summarisation as the detail is not required. This has an effect on the model as shown in Figure 4.51.

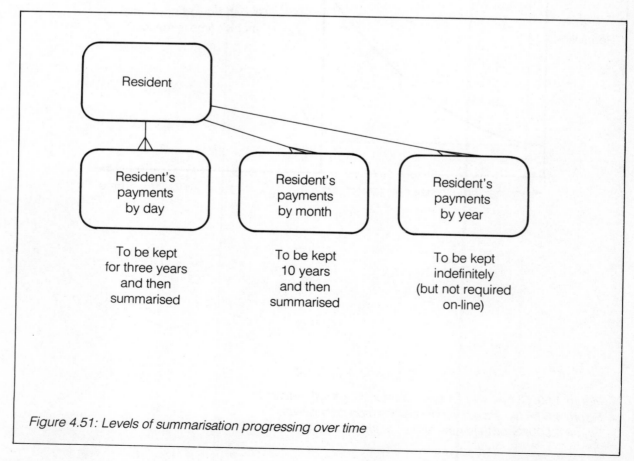

Figure 4.51: Levels of summarisation progressing over time

Thus, considering 'longevity' can have an effect on the model by causing the creation of extra *derived* entity types to meet the need for greater summarisations over time.

2.7.5.3 *Hints and guidelines*

It is possible that certain attribute types of an entity type are not required for the same length of time as the entity type. If this is so, we record the longevity required for these attribute types separately and do our calculation during design accordingly. The entity type 'takes' the longevity of the attribute type with the highest longevity so that if attribute types A to D are to be kept for five years, but attribute types E and F are to be kept for 10 years, the longevity of the entity type is 10 years and we record the shorter figures of five years for attribute types A, B, C and D separately. We have no need to record the longevity details of attribute types E and F as they default to that of their owning entity type.

This will be explained in more detail in Section 4.

Relationship types

3 Relationship type deliverables (100)

A relationship type is an association between an entity type and itself or two entity types. The deliverables which must be collected during analysis, their purpose, how they are represented and any hints and guidelines relating to them are described in the following sections.

3.1 Responsibility (101)

This describes which users/analysts are allowed to see the deliverables of a certain relationship type and which analyst(s) have been given the responsibility for keeping the deliverables up to date. Thus, analyst Jill Smith may have been given the responsibility to keep the 'customer has orders' relationship type and its deliverables up to date, but all users and analysts have been given permission to see those deliverables.

The specific deliverables applicable to 'responsibility' are as follows:
- Analyst/user responsible for update/allowed to look (102)
- Date last updated/looked at (103)
- Chief/deputy (104)
- Type of access allowed (105).

These have the same meaning as those described for the entity type.

3.1.1 *Purposes*

The same purposes described for the entity type responsibility deliverable also apply to this deliverable. If we want to stop unauthorised 'tampering' with deliverables there must be a way of showing who is allowed to look at and change data and who is not. This deliverable is the way in which control is defined.

3.1.2 *Hints and guidelines*

These are the same as for the entity type.

3.2 Versions/model (106)

Model 'versions' were described earlier in Chapter 2 as one view of the business system and one model solution to the business objective under discussion. A relationship type can be used in several model versions; similarly a model version will use several relationship types, hence this deliverable records all the models in which the relationship type is found.

3.2.1 *Purpose*

Versions exist so that models can be compared during package evaluation and evaluation of existing systems.

3.2.2 *Diagrammatic conventions*

See model versions in Chapter 2.

3.3 Abbreviated name (107)

A relationship type has two 'ends', that is, it has deliverables which apply to each end rather than the complete relationship type. In particular, the names apply to the ends of the relationship rather than the association itself. However, one name must be chosen to identify the relationship type as a whole and this should be an *abbreviated* name which describes the relationship type in the form 'owner' entity type, verb, 'member' entity type. For example, customer has orders (CUST-HAS-ORDER) or patient has appointment (PAT-HAS-APPT).

3.3.1 *Purposes*

This deliverable can be used during analysis as the identifier of the relationship type and as the basis for the name of any link, set or other method of implementing the relationship type in design.

3.3.2 *Hints and guidelines*

Where restrictions on the length of the name apply in design, these must be used to control the length of the abbreviated name used in analysis. For example, IDMS (Cullinet) restricts set name lengths to 16 characters, hence the abbreviated relationship name should be less than or equal to this number.

Where possible, the abbreviated entity type names should be used to form the relationship type name. If this is not possible (because of length restrictions, say), the guidelines for forming abbreviated names as given for attribute types can be used.

The name must be a simple derivation of the name in the relationship type—no 'application' or other spurious meaning should be built in, simply NOUN-VERB-NOUN. The name should not contain spaces, commas or full stops; only letters and hyphens as connectors. This makes the transition to design easier.

3.4 Definition (108)

Normally a definition is not required, as the relationship type name is self-explanatory, but some additional information may be required to clarify the extent to which the verb applies over the 'life' of the relationship type. For example, patient has operation includes the relationship established from the moment the operation is booked to the patient and continues after the operation has been undergone by the patient.

3.4.1 *Purpose*

To make it absolutely clear what is meant by the relationship type.

3.5 Relationship type end (109)

A relationship type has two 'ends' which we can describe by looking from one entity type towards the other and vice versa (see Figure 4.52).

To describe each end, we construct a 'fence' between each entity type to determine what we would see from each side. This is shown in Figure 4.53. As far as anyone looking from the patient towards the fence is concerned, the degree at the patient end is one-to-many and optional, but a person looking from the operation towards the fence sees only a mandatory one-to-one relationship.

The following deliverables are collected for each 'end':
- Name of relationship type from this end (110)
- Synonyms (other names) from this end (111)
- Basic optionality (Y/N) (112)
- Basic type of degree (1:1, 1:N, M:N) (113)
- Degree detail (114).

3.5.1 *Name of relationship type from this end (110)*

It was said earlier that relationship types do not denote direction, hence according to the verb and degree we have two choices, as follows:

1 Entity type 1 verb in active voice—entity type 2.
2 Entity type 2 verb in passive voice—entity type 1.

For example:

Hospital <u>employs</u> doctor	1:N
Doctor <u>is employed by</u> hospital	N:1
Patient <u>has appointment</u>	1:N
Appointment <u>is for</u> patient (is had by)	N:1
Operating theatre <u>is used for</u> theatre session	1:N
Theatre session <u>uses</u> operating theatre	N:1

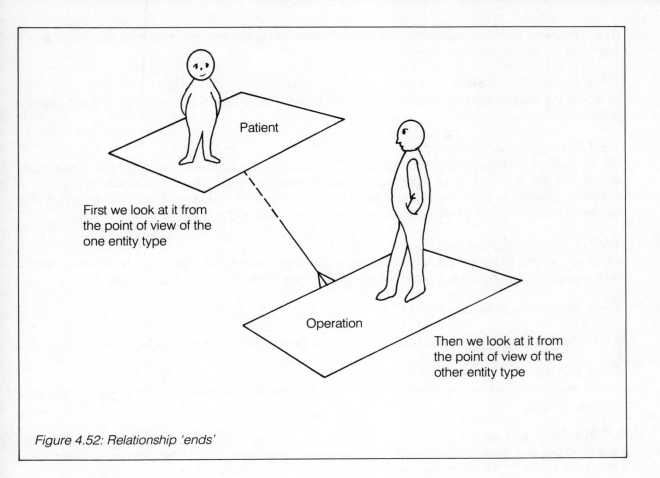

First we look at it from
the point of view of the
one entity type

Then we look at it from
the point of view of the
other entity type

Figure 4.52: Relationship 'ends'

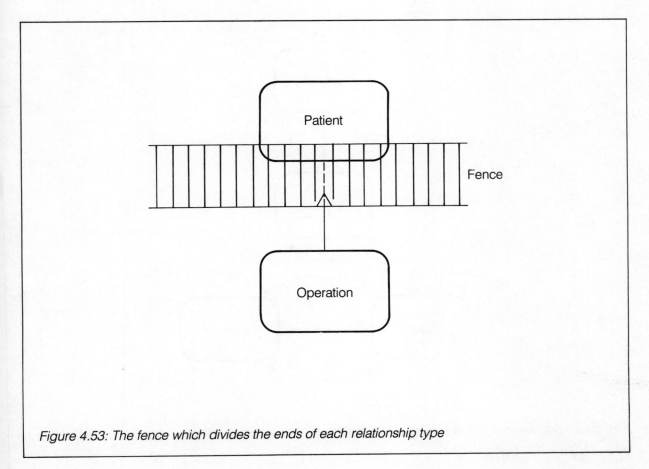

Figure 4.53: The fence which divides the ends of each relationship type

Example 1   For relationship end 'patient has operation':

Total population sampled = 8

{
Number of patients with this degree = 1
Percentage   = 12.1/2%
Degree   = 3

{
Number of patients with this degree = 1
Percentage   = 12.1/2%
Degree   = 5

{
Number of patients with this degree = 6
Percentage   = 75%
Degree   = 0

For relationship end 'operation had by patient':

Total population sampled = 8

{
Number of operations   = 8
Percentage   = 100
Degree   = 1

Example 2   For relationship end 'person owns car':

Total population sampled = 8

{
Number of people with this degree = 1
Percentage   = 12.1/2%
Degree   = 3

{
Number of people with this degree = 1
Percentage   = 12.1/2%
Degree   = 2

{
Number of people with this degree = 2
Percentage   = 25%
Degree   = 1

{
Number of people with this degree = 4
Percentage   = 50%
Degree   = 0

For relationship end 'car owned by person':

Total population sampled = 10

{
Number of cars with this degree = 7
Percentage   = 70%
Degree   = 1

{
Number of cars with this degree = 3
Percentage   = 30%
Degree   = 0

Figure 4.63: A more precise representation of relationship types having optionality and degree

2   *Number of owner entities with this degree (116):* the number of owner entities in the sample which were found to have the degree specified, that is, that specific number of 'member' entities.

3   *Percentage with this degree (117):* this equals the number of entities (116) × 100 ÷ the total population sampled (115) (this figure is derived).

4   *Degree (118):* the number of 'member' entities participating in the relationship.

There are two other (optional) deliverables which can be collected as follows:

1   *Certainty indicator (119):* this optional deliverable describes how certain the collector is that, for each degree figure collected, the figures are correct or representative. This can be used when the figures have been collected from a dubious sample or the user has had to guess rather than use actual examples.

2   *Maximum/mode indicator (120):* this indicates whether the figures are describing the maximum degree found or the mode degree found and helps to show the extreme cases which may have to be designed for.

From the point of view of the designer, it is pointless for the analyst to find the mean average degree of the relationship. It is the sum of all degree occurrences, divided by the number of occurrences. For example:

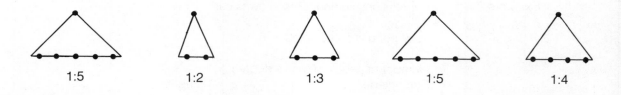

$$\text{Average} = \frac{5 + 2 + 3 + 5 + 4}{5} = \frac{19}{5} = 3\frac{4}{5} \,(!) \simeq 4.$$

The average required is the *mode* average or the *most frequently occurring degree*, because all performance calculations, design, sizing and so on will be based on this figure. The designer is more interested in the most frequent one rather than a theoretical mean which may be biased by a small number of very low or very high results. The mode indicator simply shows that the degree specified is the most frequently occurring figure. Figure 4.64 shows how to obtain this.

3.5.5.2 Diagrammatic representation
The most effective method to summarise the figures is to use a histogram—one histogram for each end as shown in Figure 4.65.

3.5.5.3 Purposes
1   *Database design/file design:* in database design we use 'sets' to implement the relationship types if we have a CODASYL-type DBMS, or we may have a link if we use IMS, TOTAL or IMAGE (see Figure 4.66).

In relational databases we embed the key of the owner into the member record, which we might also do with conventional files. It does not matter which approach we adopt or which DBMS we use however; we still have to perform the same processing (searching along the set, link and so on) when we go from owner to member.

When the DBMS has the facility to get *directly* to the members of a set via pointers, physical placement and so on (in CODASYL, IMS and TOTAL for example) processing time is not normally a problem.

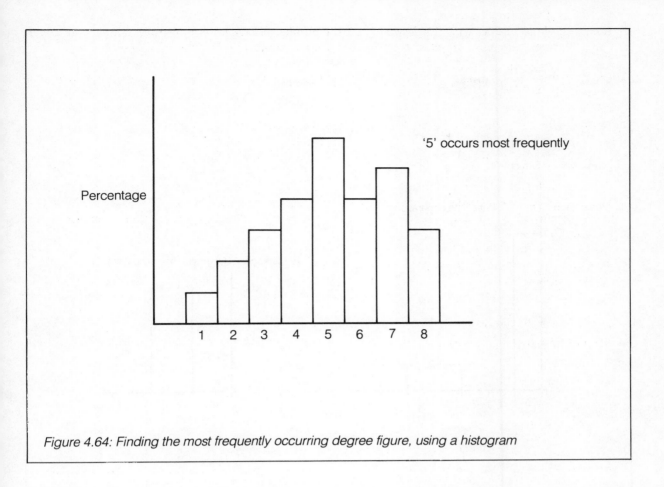

Figure 4.64: Finding the most frequently occurring degree figure, using a histogram

However, problems do occur when the degree is very large. 'Travelling' the set to process members will result in poor response times unless a way of shortening the sets is found.

Thus, the degree is used to indicate the need for intermediate indexes, 'split' sets or other design means of shortening set lengths.

Relational DBMSs create special problems, as searching for 'members' can be done through the complete population. By implication, any search is going to take a long time if the member record's population is large. For example, if all As of a B are required, all As will have to be searched (see Figure 4.67).

Some relational DBMSs use indexes to shorten the search time. Thus, 'B-key index' would have to be created for the A records.

2 *Activity analysis:* the percentage of the population having the relationship, when the relationship is optional, is used in activity analysis. Examples are shown in Figure 4.68.

We use this information to decide the best way to achieve the function. For example:

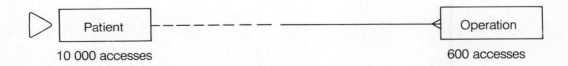

219

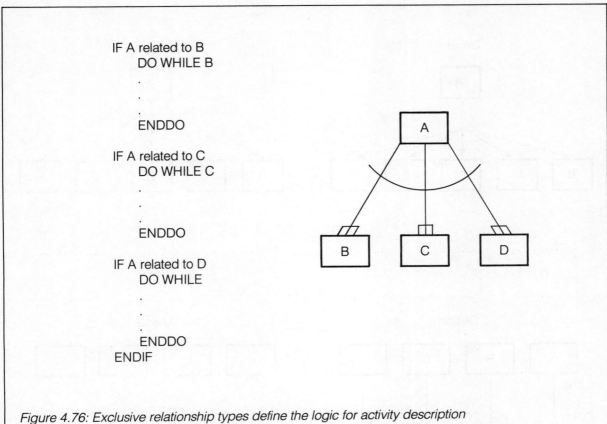

```
IF A related to B
    DO WHILE B
    .
    .
    .
    ENDDO

IF A related to C
    DO WHILE C
    .
    .
    ENDDO

IF A related to D
    DO WHILE
    .
    .
    ENDDO
ENDIF
```

Figure 4.76: Exclusive relationship types define the logic for activity description

3.6.2.1 Diagrammatic representation

The way in which inclusive relationships are depicted in the model is shown in Figure 4.79. The relationship type which must be present is shown again, as a line linking the two entity types. The relationship types, whose occurrences cannot exist unless corresponding occurrences of the first relationship type exist, are depicted as a line *at angles* to the first relationship type.

3.6.2.2 Purposes

The purposes for inclusivity are virtually the same as those for exclusivity.

3.6.2.3 Hints and guidelines

Inclusivity is a property which is nearly always caused by *events*. As we want our model to be event-dependent, we normally find that inclusivity disappears upon refinement of the model. We need to preserve the concept and diagrammatic conventions to help in the process or modelling and to enable us to record the very rare occasions when an inclusive relationship type exists which is not event-dependent.

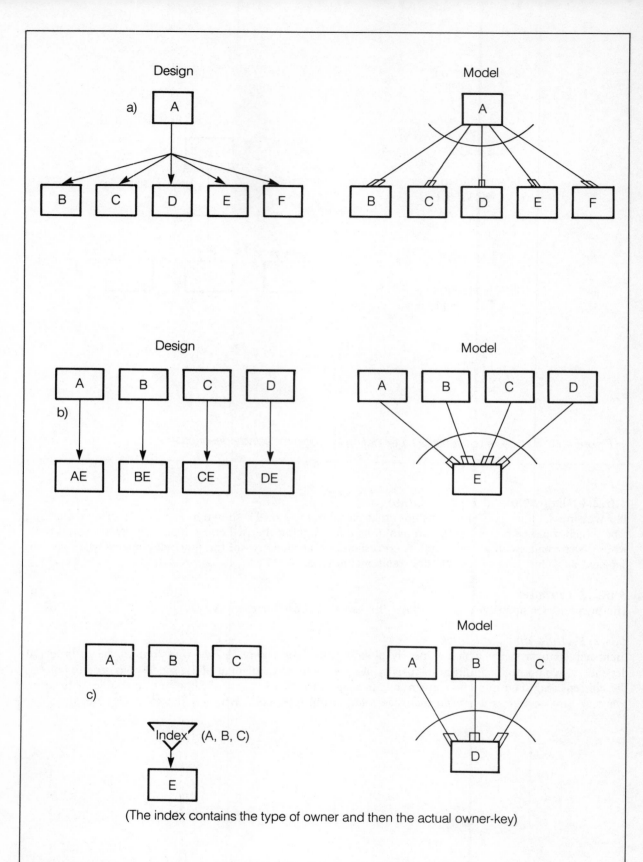

Figure 4.77: Exclusivity may result in extra record types or combined relationship types
Figure 4.77a: Two or more record types could be created but one set (CODASYL)
Figure 4.77b: False record types can be created to save pointer space
Figure 4.77c: Stand-alone index records can be created to save pointer space

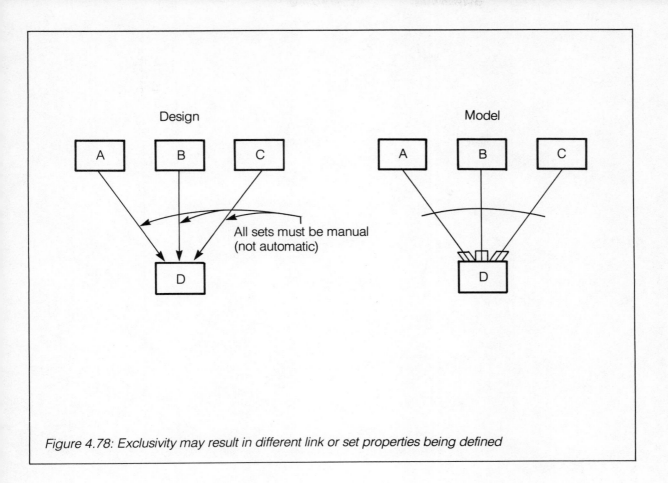

Figure 4.78: Exclusivity may result in different link or set properties being defined

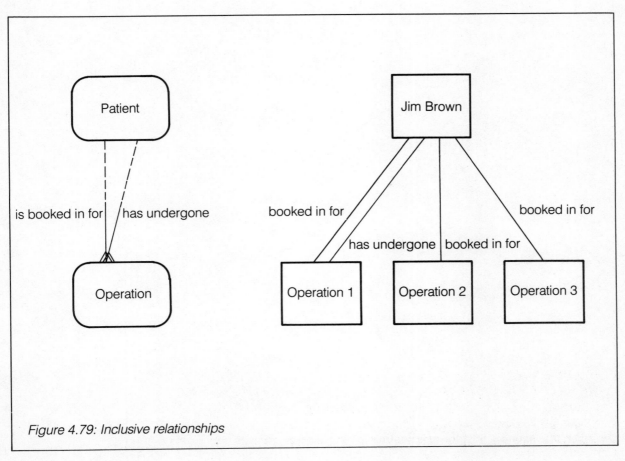

Figure 4.79: Inclusive relationships

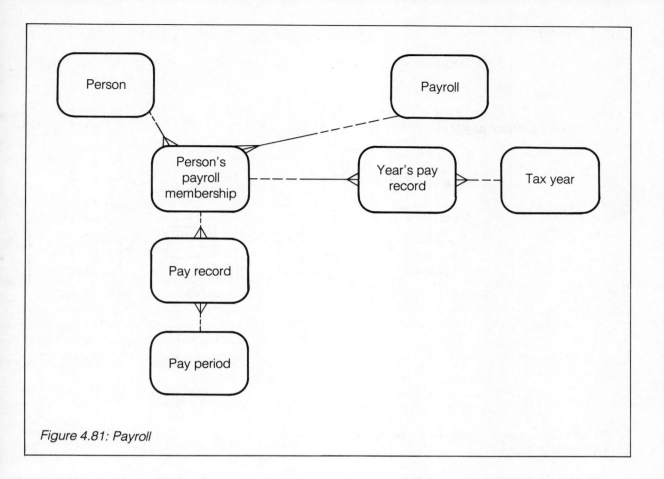

Figure 4.81: Payroll

person over time, we may have the following attribute types:
- Current name of person
- Previous name of person
- Previous but one name of person.

4.8 Entity type or subtype described (212)

A specific attribute type can describe either an entity type or an entity subtype. If it defines an entity subtype we *must* define it in relation to the entity subtype and associate it with this subtype. For example:
- Entity type: resident
- Entity subtypes: bank and non-bank
- Attribute type: name of resident (resident)
- Attribute type: bank code (bank)
- Attribute type: dispute indicator (non-bank).

Only stable entity subtypes must be used—they must not be representing stages in the entity type's life which are affected by events.

4.8.1 *Purpose*

The reason we do this is to ensure that validation is performed according to the entity subtype to which the attribute type belongs. For example, IF RESIDENT = 'BANK', DISPUTE INDICATOR = 'ZERO' (not applicable).

We also do this so that, during design, we can make a conscious decision whether to split the entity type into its subtypes for the purpose of creating record types. For example, if entity type x has attribute types 1, 2, 3, 4 and 5 (10 000 occurrences), entity subtype y has additional attribute types 6, 7, 8, 9 and 10 (2000 occurrences), whereas entity subtype z has additional attribute types 11 and 12 (8000 occurrences).

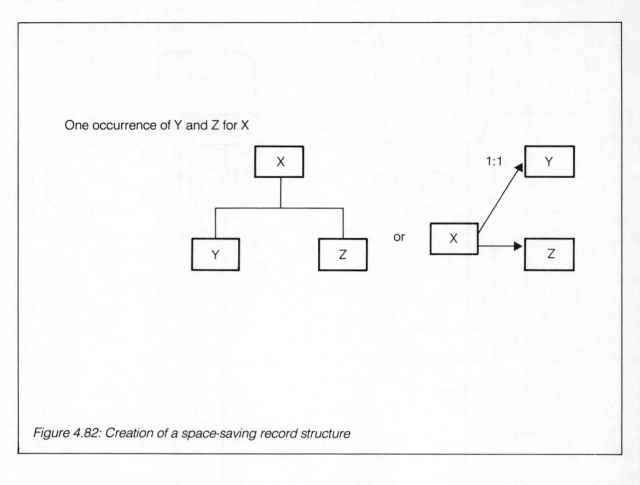

Figure 4.82: Creation of a space-saving record structure

We may create a record structure as shown in Figure 4.82 if we have fixed length records and want to save on space.

More detail on this purpose is provided under the heading of entity subtypes.

4.9 Attribute type association (213)

Attribute types may be associated with one another for the following reasons:
- They are general attribute types to which others conform
- They are redefined by others
- They are 'subtypes' of the main one (groupings of others).

Each of these different associations, and the reasons why we are interested in them, are described below.

4.9.1 *General attribute type*

This association shows which specific attribute types conform to the general definition, validation and so on which are described by a general attribute type. For example:

General attribute type   : Date
Attribute types related   : Date of birth of patient
                                : Date of death of patient
                                : Date of admission of patient to hospital
                                : Date of discharge of patient from hospital.

4.9.1.1 *Purpose*
The purpose of general attribute types is to save effort in repeatedly recording the same details. If the same validation rules are used, specific attribute types which conform to a general attribute type need only use

242

these rules and they can be defined once and subsequently be used over and over again. We need only write the slightly tighter definition applied to the specific attribute type and we have no need to include the rest of the definition as found in the general attribute type. The same is true for many other details which we collect about attribute types.

This implies that when validation rules are being incorporated into activity descriptions, the specific attribute type rules are used in addition to the rules of its owning general attribute type. Using the previous example, the format of 'date' can be constant (for example, YYMMDD) and we can apply certain constant validation rules to it. For example:

```
  Year = 00 to 99
Month = 01 to 12
   Day = 01 to 28 if month = 02 and so on
       = 01 to 31 if month = 01, 03 and so on
       = 01 to 30 if month = 09, 04, 06, 11.
```

When we have the specific attribute types of date of birth of patient for example, we can apply tighter rules *in addition* to those we have already specified. For example:

Date of birth ⩽ today's date
                         ⩾ today's date less 110 years.

4.9.2 *Group attribute types*

An attribute type can be broken down into 'smaller' attribute types which have their own definition and format. For example:

```
Date of birth—day of birth
                      —month of birth
                      —year of birth.
```

In some cases this can cover several levels - a 'hierarchy' of attribute types of more specific meaning. For example:

```
Product code—product type
                        —product number—coding system identification
                                                  —number within coding system.
```

4.9.2.1 *Purpose*
The reason for having group attribute types and sub-attribute types is so that when activities use them, we can refer to each part and the group items, without the need to refer to every individual sub-attribute type. This will carry through to design and the database design should reflect this structure.

4.9.3 *Redefines*

Used at the logical level, this has a different meaning to that used in COBOL. If one attribute type redefines another it is describing the fact that it has the same definition, is serving the same purpose and belongs to the same entity type, but its format and validation rules are different. The difference must only be in the character format chosen. If necessary, where the redefined format is actually less in characters than the redefined attribute type, the extra characters can be given a value of zero or spaced to make the length the same. Any number of attribute types can redefine one another—there is no limit. For example:

Type of identifier number coding system	99
(VAT, account number, identity number)	
Identifier number (of resident)	x(11)
—account number redefines identifier number	x(11)
—identity number redefines identifier number	9(11)
—VAT number redefines identifier number	9(11).

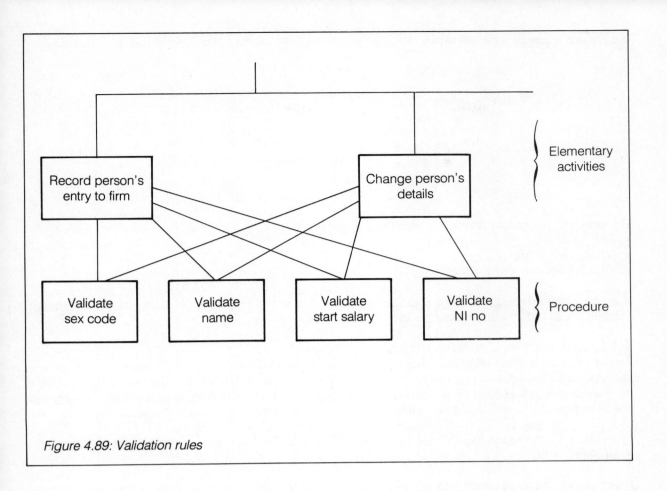

Figure 4.89: Validation rules

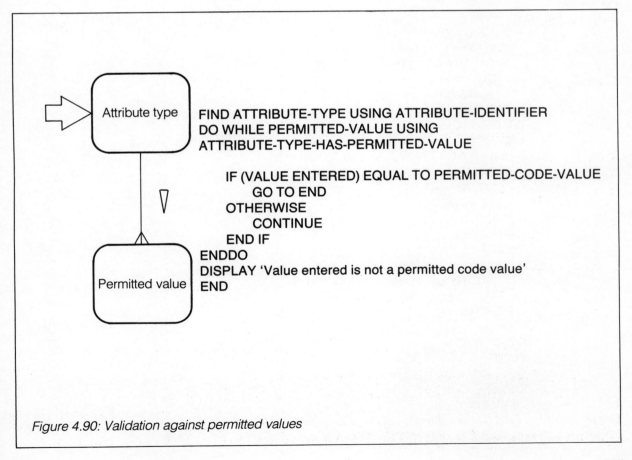

FIND ATTRIBUTE-TYPE USING ATTRIBUTE-IDENTIFIER
DO WHILE PERMITTED-VALUE USING
ATTRIBUTE-TYPE-HAS-PERMITTED-VALUE

    IF (VALUE ENTERED) EQUAL TO PERMITTED-CODE-VALUE
       GO TO END
    OTHERWISE
       CONTINUE
    END IF
ENDDO
DISPLAY 'Value entered is not a permitted code value'
END

Figure 4.90: Validation against permitted values

the chance to create external tables, we may simply have to produce this type of rule, as follows:

```
VALIDATE SEX-CODE

READ SEX-OF-PERSON

CASE 1      SEX-CODE = M
CASE 2      SEX-CODE = F
CASE 3      SEX-CODE NOT EQUAL M OR F
            DISPLAY 'sex-code invalid'
ENDCASE
```

The concept of permitted value includes the following:
- Null value
- Not known value
- Miscellaneous or other value.

If we have defined the rules for their existence correctly in our determination of these values, our general validation will either include them or exclude them if they do not exist.

4.15.1.2 *Validation against permitted value ranges*
Permitted value ranges define the ranges of quantitative or coded values which are allowed. Value ranges can be used for identifier and non-identifier attribute types and, generally speaking, are more likely to be used for quantitative rather than coded attribute types. Again, no permitted value ranges should be built into the description of the validation procedure. As with permitted values, the ranges should be held externally.

In Figure 4.91 the processing (in structured English) is at the meta-model level and the same rules apply as in Figure 4.90.

If we have no chance to create external tables, we may have to build the rules we describe into the procedure. For example:

```
READ SALARY-OF-PERSON
IF SALARY-OF-PERSON ⩽ £6000
  IF SALARY-OF-PERSON ⩾ £3000
    GO TO END
  OTHERWISE
  ENDIF
OTHERWISE
ENDIF
IF SALARY-OF-PERSON ⩽ £10 000
  IF SALARY-OF-PERSON ⩾ £7000
    GO TO END
  OTHERWISE
  ENDIF
OTHERWISE
ENDIF
IF SALARY-OF-PERSON ⩽ £15 000
  IF SALARY-OF-PERSON ⩾ £12 000
    GO TO END
  OTHERWISE
  ENDIF
OTHERWISE
ENDIF
DISPLAY 'invalid salary, not in allowed ranges'
END
```

This procedure to validate the salary, is checking it against three allowed ranges of values: £3000 to £6000, £7000 to £10 000, and £12 000 to £15 000.

256

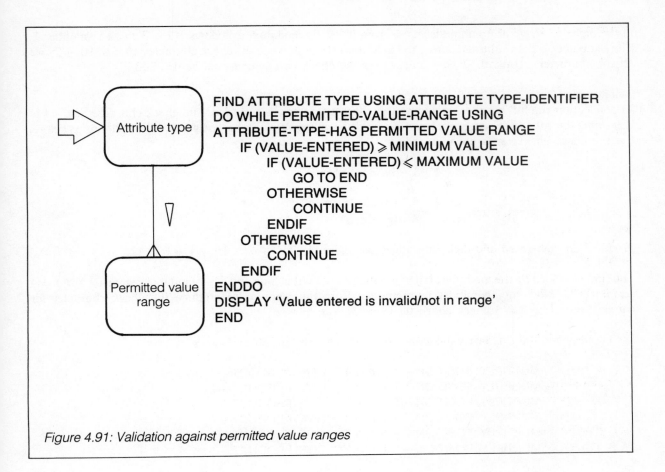

```
                 FIND ATTRIBUTE TYPE USING ATTRIBUTE TYPE-IDENTIFIER
                 DO WHILE PERMITTED-VALUE-RANGE USING
                 ATTRIBUTE-TYPE-HAS PERMITTED VALUE RANGE
   Attribute type      IF (VALUE-ENTERED) ⩾ MINIMUM VALUE
                          IF (VALUE-ENTERED) ⩽ MAXIMUM VALUE
                              GO TO END
                          OTHERWISE
                              CONTINUE
                          ENDIF
                      OTHERWISE
                          CONTINUE
                      ENDIF
  Permitted value  ENDDO
     range         DISPLAY 'Value entered is invalid/not in range'
                   END
```

Figure 4.91: Validation against permitted value ranges

4.15.1.3 *Validation against format*
This is a check that if the format defines alphabetic all the characters *are* alphabetic, if it defines numeric, they *are* numeric and so on. For example:

- If not numeric
- If not alphabetic
- If not two characters
- If negative (when should be positive).

4.15.1.4 *Check digit validation*
The analyst designs check digits at the analysis stage as part of the procedures required to ensure the validity of the information as it is recorded or transferred within the system. The method of *checking* check digits is similar to that used to derive them. The only difference is that when they are derived the last step is to add the digit to the number, but in checking the last step is to compare the numbers.

For example, given the base code 457843, we could derive the check character in the following way.

Creation
Each position of a character in the base code is given a weight (the amount by which it is multiplied to derive a product). In this example, the least significant position (right-most position) is given a weight of two, the next one and so forth with alternating values until all positions are assigned weights as follows:

```
    4   5   7   8   4   3   (base number)

    1   2   1   2   1   2   (weight)
    ───────────────────────
    4  10   7  16   4   6
```

Each character in the base number is multiplied by its weight to produce the products shown which are then added to give a sum of the digits, that is, $4 + 10 + 7 + 16 + 4 + 6 = 47$ (sum). The sum is divided by 10, which produces a quotient of four and a remainder of seven (10, the number used to divide the sum of the digits to arrive at a remainder, is referred to as the modulus) as follows: $47 \div 10 = 4$ remainder 7. The remainder is then subtracted from the modulus (10) to produce the check character; that is, $10 - 7 = 3$ (check character). Thus, the base number plus the check character would be 4578433.

Validation

In application the full number, including the check character, is recorded. The check character is used to determine the validity or consistency of the recorded number. Weights are assigned to the positions as before, but the check character is not included:

$$
\begin{array}{cccccc}
4 & 5 & 7 & 8 & 4 & 3 \quad \text{(base number)} \\
\hline
1 & 2 & 1 & 2 & 1 & 2 \quad \text{(weight)} \\
\hline
4 & 10 & 7 & 16 & 4 & 6 \quad \text{(products)}
\end{array}
$$

Products are generated and digits are added as before: $4 + 10 + 7 + 16 + 4 + 6 = 47$.

The sum is divided by the modulus (10) to produce a quotient of four and a remainder of seven: $47 \div 10 = 4$ remainder 7. Now the remainder is subtracted from the modulus to produce the check character for comparison: $10 - 7 = 3$ check character (3) = 3? Yes!

We could generalise this last validation step in structured English as follows:

```
MULTIPLY POSITION—1 BY 1 TO GIVE PRODUCT—1
MULTIPLY POSITION—2 BY 2 TO GIVE PRODUCT—2
MULTIPLY POSITION—3 BY 1 TO GIVE PRODUCT—3
MULTIPLY POSITION—4 BY 2 TO GIVE PRODUCT—4
MULTIPLY POSITION—5 BY 1 TO GIVE PRODUCT—5
MULTIPLY POSITION—6 BY 2 TO GIVE PRODUCT—6

ADD PRODUCT—1 AND PRODUCT—2 AND PRODUCT—3
AND PRODUCT—4 AND PRODUCT—5 AND PRODUCT—6
TO GIVE SUM-OF-PRODUCTS
DIVIDE SUM-OF-PRODUCTS BY 10 TO GIVE QUOTIENT
MULTIPLY QUOTIENT BY 10 TO GIVE RESULT
SUBTRACT RESULT FROM SUM-OF-PRODUCTS TO GIVE REMAINDER
SUBTRACT REMAINDER FROM 10 TO GIVE CHECK-CHARACTER
IF CHECK-CHARACTER IS NOT EQUAL TO POSITION—7
  Display 'Error'
OTHERWISE
ENDIF
END
```

4.15.2 *Summary*

There are only four types of general validation rules which we can apply against attribute types, as follows:

1 The permitted value.
2 The permitted range.
3 The format.
4 The check digit tests.

Any validation which involves combinations of attribute type values is dependent on the valid state allowed. We see this in activity analysis when we study the concept of 'state' (the valid stages in the entity life-cycle, expressed as the combinations of attribute values which are allowed to exist and those which must exist before an activity can act).

4.16 Derivation rules (224)

The categories of concept for two classes of attribute types—basic and derived—were described in Chapter 3.

To ensure that a derived attribute type is consistent, it must always be derived in the same way. However, it can be argued that the method of derivation is part of the definition of a derived attribute type—a different method of derivation will produce a different attribute type.

More than one activity may need or produce the attribute type and in order to keep the derivation consistent, *the rules* should be defined as a standard procedure to be used by each elementary activity which requires it.

This is much the same principle as that used for validation rules, except that derivation may depend on/use other attribute types. The rule is defined once and can then be 'called' by higher level activities.

Derivation rules can be defined using structured English as follows:

Example 1

TOTAL-SALARY-FOR-PAY RECORD = TOTAL-ANNUAL-SALARY DIVIDED BY
NO-OF-PAY-PERIODS-IN-YEAR

Example 2

ADD (TOTAL-SALARY-FOR-PAY-PERIOD AND
TOTAL-ADDITIONAL-PAYMENTS-FOR-PAY-PERIOD AND
TOTAL-BONUS-FOR-PAY-PERIOD AND
TOTAL-ALLOWANCES-FOR-PAY-PERIOD) TO GIVE
TOTAL-GROSS-SALARY-FOR-PAY-PERIOD

Example 3

SUBTRACT (TOTAL-TAX-FOR-PAY-PERIOD AND
TOTAL-NATIONAL-INSURANCE-FOR-PAY-PERIOD AND
TOTAL-DEDUCTION-FOR-PAY-PERIOD) FROM
TOTAL-GROSS-SALARY-FOR-PAY-PERIOD TO GIVE
TOTAL-NET-SALARY-FOR-PAY-PERIOD

Example 4

ADD 1 TO NUMBER-OF-ENQUIRIES-THIS-YEAR

The first three examples show the dependency between attribute types for derivation. The last example shows how an attribute type may not depend on any other for its existence. In this case it is derived by adding one to the total each time an 'enquiry' is made. Included within the category of derivation rules is an important group which covers *check digit* derivation.

When utilised, the check character feature provides the capability to detect most clerical or recording errors. These errors are categorised in four types as follows:

1 Transposition errors (1234 recorded as 1243).
2 Double transposition errors (1234 recorded as 1432).
3 Transcription errors (1234 recorded as 1235).
4 Random errors (1234 recorded as 2243) which are multiple combinations of transposition and transition errors.

When the number of characters in a proposed code exceeds four and when this will be for the identification of major subjects (for example organisations, projects, materials, individuals), consideration should be given to the addition of a check character to avoid recording errors. The use of a self-checking code avoids unnecessary problems of posting data to the wrong record and providing misinformation. Several techniques are employed to generate the check character, each with its advantages and disadvantages based upon the degree of reliability essential to the particular application. The general method of forming check digits is as follows:

1 Multiply each digit of the original number by chosen numbers which are called *weightings*. Any weightings may be used, but it is usual to adjust them so that they are lower than the modulus.

2 Add the products of the multiplication.

When we need to calculate volumes during design we will use these figures. For example, suppose that the initial length of the record is 200 bytes and after five years it is reduced to 100 bytes. The actual bytes required will then be as follows:

$$200 \times 5 \times \text{occurrences per year (say 4000)}$$
$$+ \ 100 \times 5 \times \text{occurrences per year (say 4000)}$$
$$= 4\,000\,000 + 2\,000\,000$$
$$= 6\,000\,000 \text{ bytes.}$$

We only calculate total volumes during design. The volume figures and longevity remain separate so that we have not lost our 'base' data. Then, if the user changes his mind, we can change the longevity without affecting the volumes and vice versa.

4.17.3 *Summary*

Longevity describes how long occurrences of the attribute types are to be kept where this is different from the owning entity type, and is decided by reference to the user. It is used in conjunction with the 'total occurrences' information to calculate actual volumes during design and is used to create the 'archiving' and deletion activities.

Permitted values

Design mapping

6 Documenting existing and proposed designed systems/mapping to analysis concepts

To understand this section, the reader must have an appreciation of what 'design' is. It is the process whereby the analysis deliverables are mapped onto the design deliverables (the means by which a system can be implemented). If there were no limitations on hardware performance and cost, software flexibility, power and adaptability, the design deliverables would be almost one-for-one with the analysis deliverables. Our database design would look like the entity model, our system design would have the same program specifications as elementary function specifications. However, these restrictions do exist; hence design, as a step in the life-cycle, is necessary. A designer effectively decides on the mechanisms by which the analysis model will be implemented, taking into account the current restrictions of hardware, software and 'people'.

There are many design concepts and deliverables, but in the following section *only those of interest to the analyst during analysis* will be described. Furthermore, this only covers the design deliverables by which the data analysis concepts are mapped. The design deliverables for the *activity* concepts are not covered in this book. The design concepts covered here are as follows:
- Data item
- Record type
- File type
- Use of record types by file types
- Mapping of file types onto physical storage media
- Number of records in the 'physical' files
- Set/link
- Mapping of analysis deliverables to design concepts.

No purposes, hints and guidelines or diagrammatic representation sections will be given for the concept of design, as the description given is primarily to ensure that the analyst records the correct facts. These sections will be added when the mapping of analysis to design concepts is discussed, as at this stage it is the *mapping* which is the main objective of the analyst.

There are three main purposes for recording the mapping which the analyst should bear in mind and which may help to put this whole section into perspective. These are as follows:

1 Evaluation of packages (both application and software).
2 Conversion—the planning of conversion from old to new systems.
3 Problems—the identification of problem areas at all stages of analysis *before* design starts.

From an analyst's point of view, the only design deliverables he is likely to be interested in during analysis are those that already exist. These may take the form of proposed solutions; for example, application packages from external vendors, in-house packages or standard systems. The other type of system is the *in situ* designed system. Thus, when mapping from analysis deliverables to the design deliverables, the analyst may be mapping to *many* 'systems'. As a consequence, the documentation of data items, record types and so on, may have to cover a large number of 'possibilities' (see Figure 4.101).

As an aid, the entity model of the design concepts and their relationship with the analysis concepts is shown in Chapter 5. It may be of use to refer to this model to put the description into context.

6.1 Data item (300)

A data item (also variously called a record element, data group, data aggregate element, data element and field) is a type of container within a record type which has a specific format and position within the record type and a specific definition. It is effectively the means by which an attribute type is implemented. It may also be the means by which a relationship type is implemented (in relational systems an 'embedded key' is effectively implementing a relationship type). The only deliverables which are of interest to the analyst are as follows:

1 *Name (301):* the name given within the record type—its identifier. For example BI-GPBUP-99 , BI-SEX-LD , LM-D-BIRT.

2 *Descriptive name (302):* the full name which describes what the data item holds. For example, name of patient.

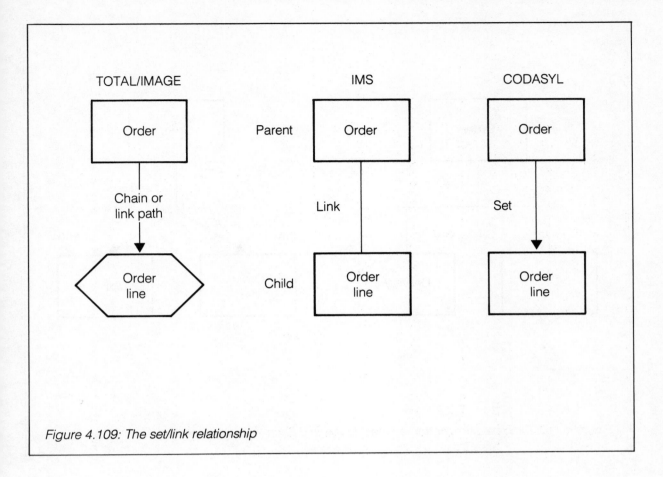

Figure 4.109: The set/link relationship

The set/link is represented by various means within a record type, as follows:

- Pointers (CODASYL)
- Sequence and pointers (IMS)
- Embedded keys (relational systems, conventional files)
- Sequence and repetition (on forms and other clerical devices).

Just as in analysis, sets/links have an implied 'owner' and 'member'. In Figure 4.109 the order is the owner and the order line is the member. A set/link is the implementation of a relationship type and the analyst requires the following deliverables:

1 *Name (801):* the name which identifies the set or link. For example, S-ORD-ORD-LN. If no name exists (for example in clerical systems or IMS), one will have to be invented.

2 *Full descriptive name (802):* a descriptive name which fully describes the link. For example, order has order lines.

3 *End (903):* just as with relationship types, sets and links have 'ends', but they can have two *or more* 'ends' (see Figure 4.110).

6.4.1 *Responsibility (804)*

This specifies the designer who is responsible for updating details of the set or link. Where access is to be restricted, the jobs which are allowed access are also given. If there are no 'look' restrictions, this implies that all may look.

6.5 Implementation (900)

An implementation is a 'copy' of a system or a defined implementation of that system. The implementation may have no relationship to the organisation of a business; it may simply be a reflection of past needs

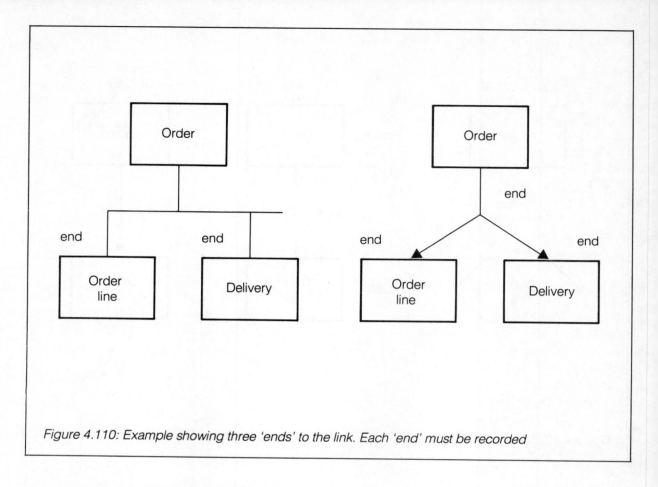

Figure 4.110: Example showing three 'ends' to the link. Each 'end' must be recorded

which dictated that the system would be implemented for a certain part of the business. It can only be defined precisely if it is known which population of entities of all types are covered and what criteria are used to define membership (this concept was also discussed in relation to the file implementation concept).

The deliverables are as follows:
- Name—identifying name (901)
- Full descriptive name (902)
- Responsibility (903)—designer responsible for updating the implementation details and enforcing restrictions on 'looking'.

6.6 System (computer) (1000)

The final concept used in design is that of a computer 'system'—a grouping of program types and clerical procedures which satisfy some given purpose. A system may be an application or software package or an 'existing' system. As already described, each 'system' can have a number of 'implementations', as follows:
- Payroll 'system'
  —south payroll system
  —north payroll system
  —north-west payroll system.

6.6.1 Usage (1001)

A system can use a number of file types, record types and data items and it is possible that these are used by more than one system—particularly if a 'database' approach has been adopted. Therefore, the usage of these should be recorded in order that a 'system' can be defined (in terms of what data it uses) and comparisons made between systems.

The deliverables which are required about a system are as follows:

1 *Proposed/current (1002):* this is an indication of whether the system is proposed as a possible solution (for example, a package or 'outside' system) or is a current system (*in situ*) which is likely to be converted. The distinction must be based on whether the recording of a system's existence is for the purpose of evaluation only (proposed) or for conversion (current).

2 *Name of system (1003):* this is the name given to a package by its vendor or the internal name given by the system team or user.

3 *Short name (abbreviated) (1004):* this is used as the identifier of the system.

4 *Description of system (1005):* this is a description of the major purposes of the system; its objective and features (as described by the vendor or by the system team or user). An attempt should be made to relate it to the objectives as identified during activity analysis.

6.7 Mapping of analysis to design concepts (1100)

It should now be clear what concepts are used in design to enable the analysis results to be implemented. When re-design (the replacement of the existing system) is started, the analysis deliverables are used to create a new design and mapping can be recorded during this process.

During analysis, however, it is the mapping to existing and already designed systems which is undertaken. According to the number of systems being mapped, the process will occur from once to any number of times.

6.7.1 *Purposes*

There are four main purposes for mapping the analysis to the present or proposed system designs, as follows:

1 Package evaluation—to see whether the package meets requirements.

2 Conversion planning. When we do conversion we must know on which master or transaction files data is presently represented, in order that:
- At the time of implementation, one or more of these files can be used for conversion
- When the system is in production, it is known which files must be updated from the new files if duplicate data is held for the purpose of transition in phases from new to old
- We know which files can be replaced by the new files when they are designed.

3 Highlighting problems with existing systems (planning) to show where they are deficient.

4 Helping in the analysis ('bottom-up' analysis).

6.7.2 *Software/package evaluation*

There are two types of evaluation which can be helped by using mapping, as follows:

1 The evaluation of an application package (a package which aims to model some part of the business).

2 The evaluation of 'software tools', which aim to support a part of the DP person's job by providing tools for the designer or programmer.

6.7.2.1 *Packages*
It is highly unlikely that any firm will ever find a package which completely models its business system, unless that business system is 'common', because it has to interface with government or other firms or because it must follow standard rules laid down by a professional body (for example, accounting rules). Many application package vendors 'hide' the data structure and functions which

their package supports in cloudy descriptions of how wonderful it is and how it is operated, but never in terms of what it does, divorced from the technical aspects, and what data can be recorded, divorced from the concept of files. Thus, the first stage in the evaluation of any package is to extract the following:

- The entity model supported
- The attribute types supported.

In other words, a bottom-up analysis to derive the functions from the programs, the data from the file and records, and the resultant entity model. Then we can compare the picture which the vendor has of our world and the picture we have of our world (inevitably, they will not match). This is done by comparing the *two models* —that required by the business and the one extracted from the package. Each deliverable is compared for a match. For example:

- What attribute types are missing?
- What entity types are missing?
- What relationship types are missing?
- What entity types are present but not needed?
- What relationship types are present but not needed?
- What attribute types are present but not needed?

During detailed analysis we compare such things as the following:

- Is the attribute type coding acceptable to users?
- Have null values and default values been taken into account?
- Can the files cope with the volumes of entity type we are likely to obtain?
- Can the system provide the level of privacy/security required?

We produce a long list which simply compares deliverables. Two examples are shown in Figures 4.111 and 4.112. In the first example, we are testing for *match* (that is, where the two sets of requirements statements match), but we can also assess whether the package does what it says it will. In Figure 4.111, this software package is likely to be rejected. In Figure 4.112 the package does not recognise the existence of properties or clinic sessions.

At the strategy analysis stage we match the strategy analysis deliverables; at the overview stage the overview deliverables. If the package passes these tests, we go on to evaluate it using the detailed analysis deliverables. We then go through the list of comparison of deliverables and assess where the deficiencies are and whether they are serious. From the list of missing or inadequate activity, data and so on, we can deduce how long it will take to amend the package to meet our requirements and then compare this with the cost of developing the same system ourselves. For example:

Package

Cost of package	£120 000 (one-off)
Cost of vendor support	£ 60 000 per year
Likely cost of enchancements (from vendor)	£ 20 000 per year
Machine and equipment running costs	£ 40 000 per year
	£240 000 in first year
	£120 000 in subsequent years

Estimated cost of amending system to meet our requirements	= £ 90 000 (one-off)
Additional running costs	£ 10 000 per year
Total cost of package	£240 000 + £100 000 = £340 000 in first year
Plus an annual running cost	£120 000 + £ 10 000 = £130 000

Own system

Cost of development	= £240 000
Machine and equipment running cost	= £ 30 000 per year

Results of analysis of hospital system	Analysis of the 'too good to be true' hospital administration package
1 Entity type: Property	Not present
2 Entity type: Patient	Present
– Volumes : 150 000 (maximum)	Can only cater for 10 000
3 Relationship type: Patient has property	Not present ˙
4 Relationship type: Patient has appointment	Implemented by using embedded key in appointment record but function does not control consistency, eg if patient removed no check is made that appointment cancelled

Figure 4.111: Example of evaluation of software

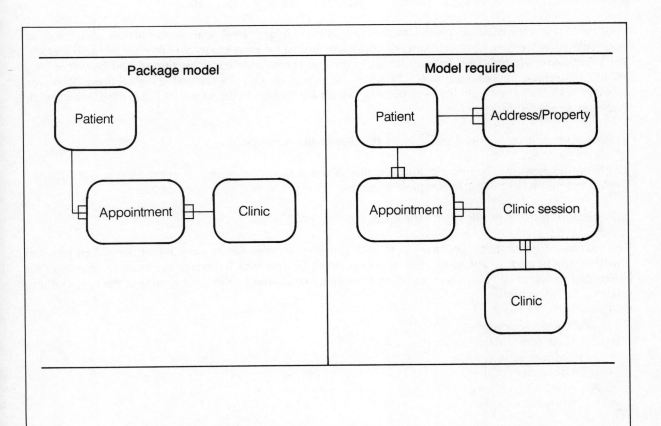

Figure 4.112: Evaluation of a package – model comparison

297

This makes our system a lot cheaper even though, at first sight, it appears to be more expensive. Thus, software/package evaluation involves (in part) the matching of *what is required* to *what the package provides*. Both application packages and systems software must be evaluated for their match against the functional and data requirements and their suitability for the types of application being considered.

6.7.2.2 *Software*

In the early days of the development of software tools, 'sort' and 'merge' utilities were the first to emerge. Now there are DBMSs, report generators, program generators and so on. The functions of project development are effectively becoming more automated and we may soon see packages for database design or systems architecture construction which use the results of analysis. We may think that these are totally different, but it is important to remember that DP has become just as much a part of the business as any other function and the arbitrary split which DP professionals make when talking about the automation of *other* people's jobs when compared with *their own*, is very short sighted.

6.7.3 *Conversion planning*

To be able to convert from one system to another it is essential to know which file, record and system holds the most reliable and up to date data on an entity or an attribute of that entity. For example, if we had an entity type 'patient' and the attribute types sex, date of birth, name (current), current temperature-of-patient and current state of health-of-patient, the sex, date of birth and name may be held in an enormous number of separate file/record types. For example:

- Admissions file
- Physiotherapy record file
- Discharge department file
- Ward file
- Central patient record file.

Joe Smith's details, for example, may be held on one, a number or all of these files. Conversion planning involves making a decision on the following:

- Which record types and file types hold the most reliable data or an entity type
- From which of those available we are to obtain the data of a single entity.

Thus we have a number of 'candidate sources' at the 'design' level and at the actual occurrence or implementation level we have to choose the definitive source for each group of entities or *partitioned* group. Therefore, conversion planning must ultimately revolve around the 'entity partitions' and how they map on to the present 'record partitions'. This will be explained fully in the following sections. However, conversion planning not only involves deciding which file should be the source of data, but it involves the following decisions also:

1 Which file can be removed/replaced by the files of the new system.

2 Which old files must be updated from the files of the new system once it is in production—if duplicate data has to be held because complete transition from old to new was not possible.

6.7.4 *Highlighting problems of the existing system*

The purpose of highlighting problems is to help plan for whether the existing system should be replaced entirely, only in part or not at all. The technique used for this task is exactly the same as that used for evaluating packages (that is, a bottom-up analysis and comparison of every deliverable of the two resulting models). For example:

1 At attribute type level
   - Is format correct/large enough?
   - Are codes adequate?
   - Is security correct?
   - Are null values allowed for?
   - Is default value correct?

2 At entity type level
   - Is entity allowed for?

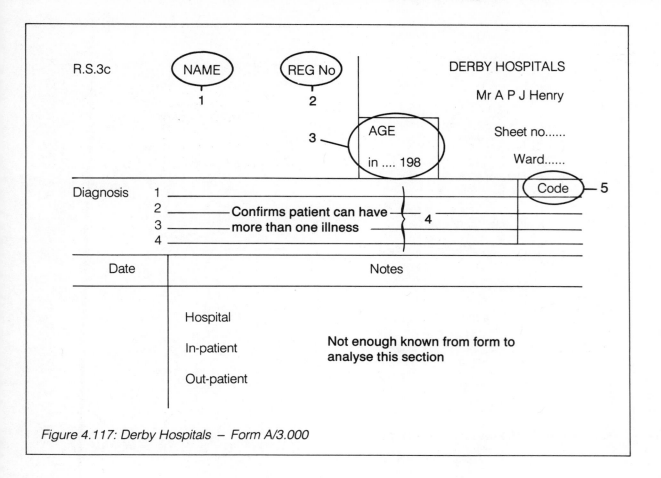

R.S.3c

1 NAME
2 REG No
3 AGE in 198

DERBY HOSPITALS

Mr A P J Henry

Sheet no......

Ward......

Diagnosis
1 _____
2 _____
3 _____
4 _____

Confirms patient can have more than one illness

4

Code — 5

Date

Notes

Hospital

In-patient

Out-patient

Not enough known from form to analyse this section

Figure 4.117: Derby Hospitals – Form A/3.000

Generally speaking, where 'transaction files' contain duplicated data (sorted data or data at intermediate stages of validation), there is no point in recording the mapping of attribute types to data items—it is a waste of effort.

6.9 Code mapping (1103)

An attribute type may have one or more permitted values or value ranges. These may be code values, quantitative values or simply a fixed narrative value. Similarly, data items also have permitted values or value ranges.

To obtain trouble-free conversion, the mapping between the values used in analysis and that in design should normally be one-for-one. Unfortunately, this is not always the case and to highlight where problems will occur, the mapping between codes at the analysis and design stages is required. This is also useful for evaluation of packages, as mentioned earlier, to see whether the package is capable of supporting the values required. The table produced can be used as the basis for automatic conversion if necessary. One permitted attribute value or range may have been implemented as one (or more) data item code value—this will cause no problems in conversion. Conversely, a data item code value may map onto more than one attribute value and this is where problems will occur, as conversion cannot then be automatic.

6.9.1 Diagrammatic representation

A matrix which shows the mapping values can be produced. If a design value maps onto more than one analysis value from different attribute types, a matrix like that shown in Figure 4.121 can be used—one for each data item.

If attribute values map onto *more than one set of design values, but not in combination*, a table such as that shown in Figure 4.122 can be used, either one table per entity type (as in the figure) or one table per attribute type—it depends on availability of space and ease of representation.

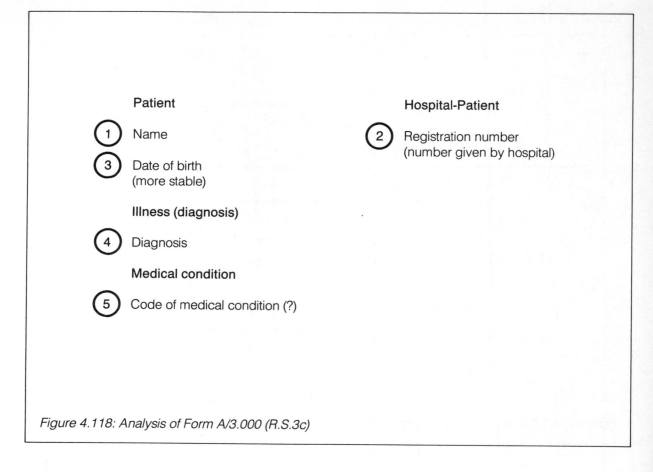

Patient

① Name

③ Date of birth
(more stable)

Hospital-Patient

② Registration number
(number given by hospital)

Illness (diagnosis)

④ Diagnosis

Medical condition

⑤ Code of medical condition (?)

Figure 4.118: Analysis of Form A/3.000 (R.S.3c)

It is assumed that an attribute value will never be formed from the *combination* of more than one data item value—that is the type of situation depicted in Figure 4.121, but where the attribute type is a classification of person code and the data items are height, sex and so on. If this situation occurs, the analyst has made an error in analysis and should re-examine his results.

The difference between Figures 4.121 and 4.122 is that one shows how a value may be mapped to others in combination (because a data item has been mapped to more than one attribute type). The other shows how a value may be mapped to others, but only because the attribute type itself has been mapped to more than one data item.

Similar tables can be produced for the valid ranges allowed.

An example is shown in Figure 4.123 which highlights where the existing system or package cannot handle the ranges required and where validation is inadequate. In this example, the current salary is required to be in the range of £5000 to £54 000. The first data item (P-SAL-CUR) only allows a range of up to £10 000; the second data item (M-SALARY) allows too great a range for effective validation. The third data item (P-SALY) has the correct lower limit, but its upper limit is too low. The date of birth attribute type is mapped to I-DAT-BIRTH, which has too high a lower range value and too low an upper range value. Data item I-DAT-BIRTH allows a wide range of values, but the dates are *invalid*.

Tables such as these can show where the data within the file is likely to be totally unreliable because the integrity checks are ineffective or non-existent. Thus, a *possible* data item may be rejected once these tables have been studied more closely. Therefore, the tables have an additional purpose in helping to decide on the *source* of an attribute type.

6.10 Entity mapping (1105)

Record types or 'group' data items are the means by which an entity type is represented in design terms. A record type may contain many entity types, for example an 'order' record type may be created which

306

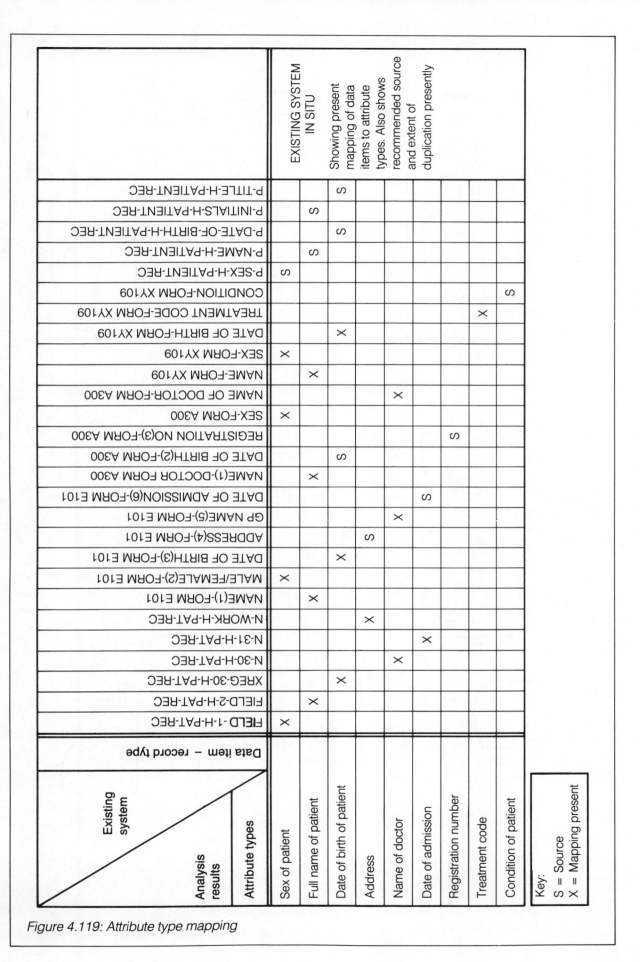

Data item – record type	Sex of patient	Full name of patient	Date of birth of patient	Address	Name of doctor	Date of admission	Registration number	Treatment code	Condition of patient
FIELD-1-H-PAT-REC	X								
FIELD-2-H-PAT-REC		X							
XREG-30-H-PAT-REC			X						
N-30-H-PAT-REC					X				
N-31-H-PAT-REC						X			
N-WORK-H-PAT-REC				X					
NAME(1)-FORM E101		X							
MALE/FEMALE(2)-FORM E101	X								
DATE OF BIRTH(3)-FORM E101			X						
ADDRESS(4)-FORM E101				S					
GP NAME(5)-FORM E101					X				
DATE OF ADMISSION(6)-FORM E101						S			
NAME(1)-DOCTOR FORM A300		X							
DATE OF BIRTH(2)-FORM A300			S						
REGISTRATION NO(3)-FORM A300							S		
SEX-FORM A300	X								
NAME OF DOCTOR-FORM A300					X				
NAME-FORM XY109		X							
SEX-FORM XY109	X								
DATE OF BIRTH-FORM XY109			X						
TREATMENT CODE-FORM XY109								X	
CONDITION-FORM XY109									S
P-SEX-H-PATIENT-REC	S								
P-NAME-H-PATIENT-REC		S							
P-DATE-OF-BIRTH-H-PATIENT-REC			S						
P-INITIALS-H-PATIENT-REC		S							
P-TITLE-H-PATIENT-REC			S						

EXISTING SYSTEM IN SITU

Showing present mapping of data items to attribute types. Also shows recommended source and extent of duplication presently

Key:
S = Source
X = Mapping present

Figure 4.119: Attribute type mapping

307

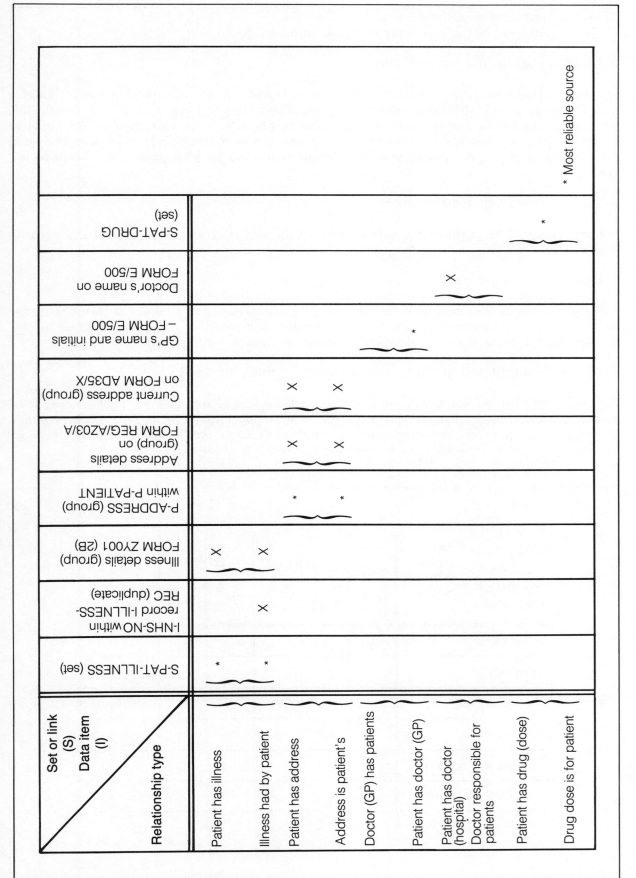

Figure 4.130: Matrix showing relationship types implemented using data items on forms or computer records and by using sets or links

6.11.1.2 *Hints and guidelines*
The same hints apply as those for entity types and attribute types.

6.12 Entity group mapping (1109)

At strategic levels, the only data analysis information available is the entity type group or 'subject' area. For the purposes of *strategic planning*, the mapping between these subject areas and (very loosely) the file types in each system must be shown. A subject area may be available on more than one file type and, conversely, a file type can hold more than one subject area. It is possible that file types relate to no subject areas and, conversely, subject areas exist for which no system has yet been designed and hence no file types exist.

6.12.1 *Diagrammatic representation*

One matrix should be produced *per system*, to which the subject areas can be mapped as shown in Figure 4.131.

6.12.2 *Hints and guidelines*

This table is used at a strategic level for the evaluation of packages, but it cannot be used directly for conversion planning. However, it is the *basis* of conversion, as it provides an indication of where to look at more detailed stages. Therefore, the mapping should be recorded for the existing system too.

6.13 Record partitioning/entity type partitioning mapping (1111)

Each entity type can be 'partitioned'—that is, its population can be split between organisational units according to logical criteria. In a previous section the example chosen was Joe Smith's works, where certain entity types—customer, address—were *shared corporately* and others—orders, order lines, products, stock, stock locations and so on—were split between the Pipe and Tool Divisions.

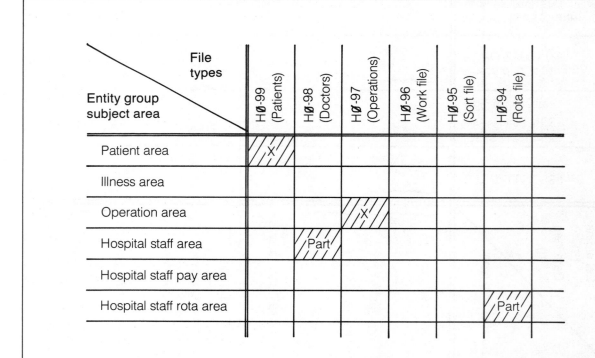

Figure 4.131: Evaluation of the 'Too good to be true' hospital administration system', showing mapping of subject areas to the package's file types

318

In order to ascertain the level of duplication, these partitions must be mapped to the partitions which occur in the files *at present. Only at this level can we ascertain whether duplicated data actually exists and therefore plan conversion.*

A certain level of duplication was identified earlier by showing where the criteria for the partitioning of record types across file types would cause duplication—for example, because of unstable criteria or record types which are duplicated across file types within the same implementation. The aim of mapping present record partitioning to required entity type partitioning is to highlight where the *existing* system duplicates data or does not provide the partitioning required. Also, it is only at this level that the *source* can be identified to cover all entities of a population.

6.13.1 *Diagrammatic representation*

A matrix is constructed like that shown in Figure 4.132. Entity types, split by organisational unit and partitioning criteria, are listed on one axis and the system implementation record type, and thus partitioning criteria, are split on the other. The criteria used for splitting the entity type can then be compared across implementations and systems. For example, when the customer is corporate and all are required there is duplication across implementations as the Pipe and Tool Divisions and Joe Smith's office each hold a file of all customers and customer addresses. Orders are duplicated *within* an implementation in the Tool Division and *across* implementations as Joe Smith also keeps a copy of tool and pipe orders.

An alternative method is to show the problem *by entity type* as shown in the hospital example in Figure 4.133. Conversion planning can only be controlled effectively at this level, as there may be *more than one source* for the entities of an entity type. Thus the deliverable required is source (most reliable) (1112), which gives an indication of which record types within file types and implementations are the best source. All *current* systems (not proposed) must be considered to see whether they can provide the data or not.

In Figure 4.132 there are three 'systems' and only one implementation of each with the customer details duplicated in each implementation. The implementation which is likely to contain the highest quality data must be chosen. The pipe or tool implementation will be sufficient, but probably not Joe Smith's file as he has less need to have complete and accurate data on a day-to-day basis. For complete accuracy, the data from the two implementations can be compared.

In the figure the tool orders are also duplicated within the tool implementation. The best source is likely to be the order file (6) as it is the nearest to the 'original source' of the customer. Thus, there are two rules when deciding the source for conversion, as follows:

1 Select the file which is the closest in the chain of operations/activities to the 'original' source outside the scope of study.

2 Choose data which users have a vested interest in maintaining accurately.

Where the quality of the data is poor, because of bad validation or systems controls, or where there is no obvious source of 'good data', no source can be recorded. Users may have to create data 'from scratch' and use printouts of the different alternative values available to recreate the data.

In Figure 4.133 there is massive duplication of patient details. Brightholmlee patients can occur in three separate files within the patient administration system and thus could have the same details in five records. The *criteria* used for partitioning also gives cause for alarm. A patient can be sent to more than one hospital and hence may have a maximum of 14 records. This massive duplication is wasteful and will lead to errors and inconsistencies of data.

Problems may also arise when the same entity occurs in different implementations (see Figure 4.134). For example, the Hallam Clinic system may have a record which states that J Smith is male and was born on 10/10/70, but Brightside Clinic system has a record which says that 'he' is female and was born on 10/12/70.

it is 'associated' with the entity type. For example:

		Attribute types
Entity type:	Patient	Name
		Address
		Date of birth
Subtypes:	Male patient	Nationality
:	Female patient	Number of births (total)
		Number of still-births

2.3 Attribute types may be associated to one another

This is because of the following:

1 They are a 'group' name for other attribute types. For example:
- Day of birth of person
- Month of birth of person
- Year of birth of person.

2 They have different 'formats' and are hence 'redefined'. For example:
- Identifier number X(11)
- VAT number redefines identifier number 9(6)
- Account number redefines identifier number 9(11).

3 The 'owning' attribute type is a general attribute type to which other attribute types are conforming. For example:
- General attribute type   : Date
- Associated attribute types: Date of birth of person
                                              : Date of payment.

2.4 Attribute types may have 'permitted values'

These may be code, fixed quantitative or fixed narrative values. For example:
- Attribute type   : Sex code of person
- Permitted values: M (male)
                              F (female).

Alternatively, the attribute type may have ranges of permitted values, in which case only ranges of quantitative or code values are allowed. For example a range from 200 to 500.

In both cases, the permitted value or value range is optionally related to the attribute type as it may be a design value or value range instead.

A permitted value or value range must describe an attribute type or a data item *or both* — it cannot exist on its own.

2.5 Relationship types

These are classifications of the assocations which can occur between entity types. Each relationship type has two ends. An entity type may participate in many relationship 'ends', but a relationship type 'end' only relates to one entity type. Three relationship types exist in Figure 5.2— A-B, A-C, and A-D—and each relationship type has two ends, giving six relationship type ends. Entity type A participates in three relationship type ends; entity types B, C and D each have only one end.

For each relationship type end, a number of 'degrees' may be known. This is the number of entities of that type which participate in the relationship type. From the sample of real data used to obtain the degree,

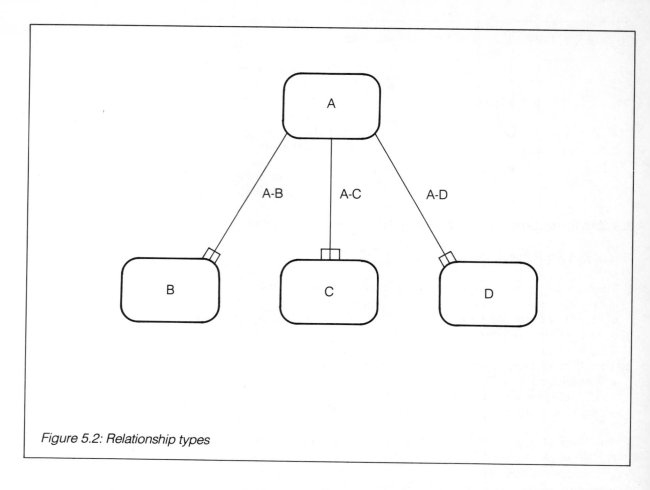

Figure 5.2: Relationship types

certain percentages of the total population may have different degrees; hence the need to hold all the degrees found. For example, using the A end of the relationship type A-B:

- 10 per cent may have a degree of 50
- 20 per cent may have a degree of 20
- 30 per cent may have a degree of 15
- 40 per cent may have a degree of 10.

Relationship type ends may be associated by being exclusively or inclusively associated (though the latter is very rare). An association must describe which relationship ends are exclusively or inclusively related (see Figure 5.3 for an example of exclusive association). The association will always describe relationship type ends which are for one entity type, but they may not be associated in this way, nor need an entity type have exclusive or inclusive relationship types with other entity types.

2.6 An entity type may have one or more identifiers, but an identifier only identifies one entity type

The identifiers are a combination of either attribute types or relationship types or both. This relationship is shown in Figure 5.4.

Thus an 'identifier' may be formed from many attribute types and/or relationship types and these may be used for many identifiers.

2.7 'Subject' areas or entity type groups

These, rather than individual entity types, may be identified during strategic analysis. They are broad areas of subject data, such as 'person data' (all data about a person; for example, qualifications, nationality, training and so on). These subject areas are broken down during overview and detailed analysis to the entity types which may not be related to any subject area. Conversely, during strategic analysis the subject groups will not be related to any entity types.

330

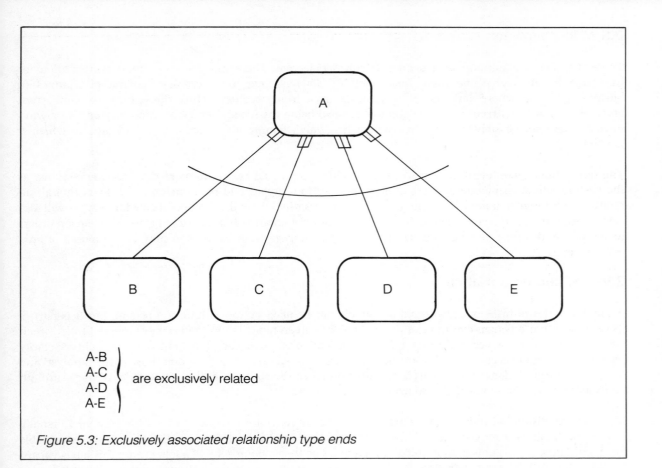

A-B
A-C
A-D
A-E } are exclusively related

Figure 5.3: Exclusively associated relationship type ends

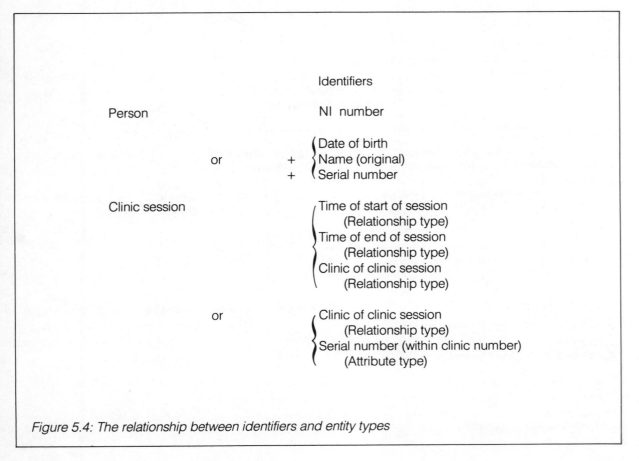

Identifiers

Person   NI number

                          ⎧ Date of birth
        or   +   ⎨ Name (original)
                  +   ⎩ Serial number

Clinic session   ⎧ Time of start of session
                          ⎪   (Relationship type)
                          ⎨ Time of end of session
                          ⎪   (Relationship type)
                          ⎩ Clinic of clinic session
                                   (Relationship type)

        or   ⎧ Clinic of clinic session
                          ⎪   (Relationship type)
                          ⎨ Serial number (within clinic number)
                          ⎩   (Attribute type)

Figure 5.4: The relationship between identifiers and entity types

2.8 Model versions

These describe one solution to a defined business objective. There may be more than one solution for the same business objective under discussion or versions may be necessary because of changes in business practice where one model is to take over from another. Thus there may be concurrent versions or non-concurrent versions (due to changes) being discussed. Therefore, each version will always have a date and, possibly, a time *from* which it is valid. It may also have a date and time *to* which it is valid.

The same entity types, attribute types or relationship types could belong to more than one version, just as the version will describe one or more entity types, attribute types and relationship types. Even though an entity type belongs to a model version, it does not necessarily follow that each of its attribute types will also belong. An attribute type may belong to one version but not another, but it cannot belong to a version unless its owning entity type also belongs. During strategic analysis a model version may be composed of only subject areas.

2.9 Jobs and organisation

A job is a series of tasks or responsibilities which can be filled by more than one person, but it is part of its definition that a person can have only one 'job' at a given time. Thus, a job is a grouping of tasks which can be executed by a person. Many types of job can exist in a company, but a useful split to clarify responsibilities and access authorisation can be made between 'user'-type jobs and those of the 'analyst' and 'designer' in the DP department. This is because control of the contents of the meta-model is made through analysts and designers and their passwords.

Business organisational units (a grouping of a number of jobs) are separate parts of the company, usually formed for administrative costing and budget reasons, and tend to be defined by the job which is responsible for them. Thus, the organisational unit should always be the responsibility of a job, even if this job is vacant (clearly, not all jobs are responsible for organisational units). An organisational unit can be 'sited' at a

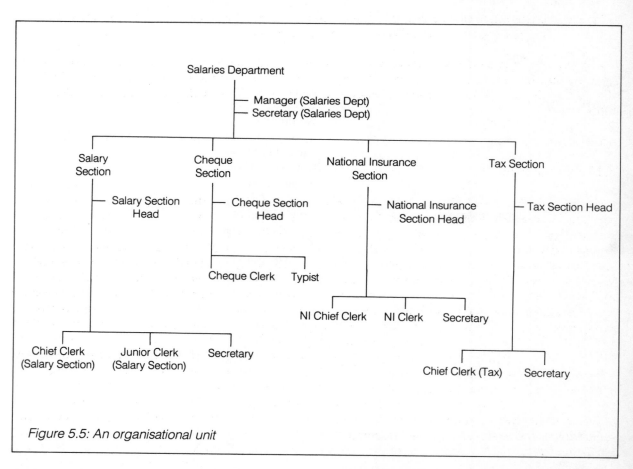

Figure 5.5: An organisational unit

particular physical location (the relationship is optional as it may not be important to know where it is placed). Similarly, a location may have many units sited there.

2.10 Allowed access/responsibility

An analyst or designer, and in some cases a user (where responsibility for an attribute type has been delegated), may be responsible for the validity of one or more entity types, attribute types and/or relationship types. Alternatively he may be responsible for the validity of a complete model, in which case he is responsible, by default, for the update of all the elements in 'membership' of that model.

Responsibility describes which job(s) are allowed to update (insert, amend and delete) elements of the meta-model. Where access to look is to be restricted, each job which is allowed access is also described, acting as a lock on access. However, where *no* lock applies it is assumed that any job may look. Jobs and their responsibilities may be described as follows:

1 A job which is responsible for the validity of an entity type also has, by default, responsibility for the identifier, distribution, partitioning, occurrences, access authorisation, archive rules and mappings of that entity type.

2 A job which is responsible for a relationship type also has, by default, responsibility for the relationship type ends, the degree, the associations and the mapping.

3 A job which is responsible for an attribute type also has, by default, responsibility for its permitted values and ranges, the mappings, association with other attribute types and the access authorisation rules.

4 A job which is responsible for a subject area also has responsibility for its mapping.

2.11 Entity type access authorisation

A job may be allowed to update details of the entities of an entity type and/or it may be allowed to look at the details of the entities of an entity type (see Figure 5.6).

Conversely, an entity type may have many jobs which are allowed to look at entities within the type or update entities of the type, although if the latter occurs the update should ideally be allocated to discrete exclusive groups of entities within the type, such that only one job updates each entity.

Access authorisation is derived from activity authorisation and the use of data by activities.

2.12 Partitioning

Each mutually exclusive, discrete and stable grouping of entities within a type, which are *naturally* partitioned at an organisational level according to stable criteria, are described using entity type partitioning. For example, the entity type customer may be 'corporate' (company, top level). Orders may be partitioned into tool and pipe orders where the partitioning is at the organisational levels of the Pipe and Tool Divisions. The criteria for splitting is whether the products ordered are for pipe or tool products (no orders can be for both). Each of these partitioned groups has 'occurrences'—the number of entities of that type—and within that partitioned group they are measured *over time*. Therefore, the corporate customer figures may appear as shown in Figure 5.7a, the pipe orders as in Figure 5.7b and the tool orders as in Figure 5.7c.

Where no partitioning occurs, because every entity type is corporate, all the occurrence figures are for the company *as a whole*. A change of user access authorisation may alter the entity type partitioning which is effectively derived from knowledge of the access authorisation required.

Where a population of entities within a type is steadily growing, archiving rules may be generated to artificially remove 'non-active' entities (those which have ended their 'life'). The values of the attribute type(s) used to signal the end of life of the partitioned entity types are required.

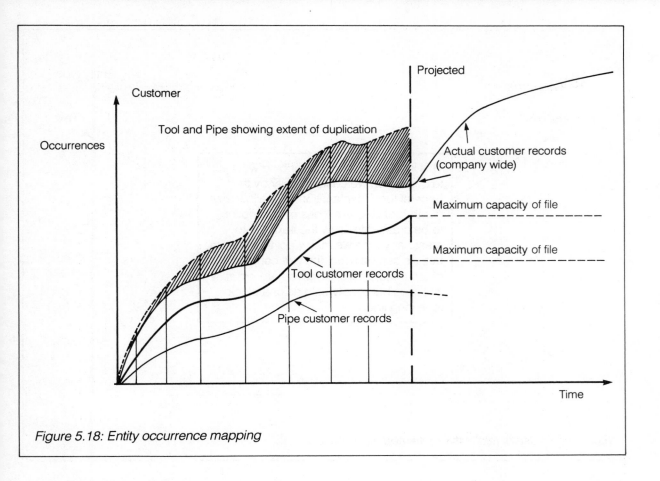

Figure 5.18: Entity occurrence mapping

3 It is about various properties of the meta-model elements which are not described in the fixed deliverable details for each concept.

It is important that the new deliverable types created using the text feature can be accessed directly; hence the 'text' type is used to classify the types of text for accessing. Any number of text types can be created according to how many need to be entered.

Thus, apart from the fixed length, fixed format deliverable types of the meta-model, we want to allow the flexibility to add variable length, variable format text on new deliverable types and classify them by their 'subject matter' (text type). This is similar to an add-on word processing facility which allows text to be linked to what it describes. It is clear that the ability to 'display' or look at the text and fixed information simultaneously must be allowed, hence the need to consider the text as part of our meta-model, not as a stand-alone 'facility'. Examples of the use of text in the meta-model are given in Figures 5.19 and 5.20.

In Figure 5.20 three new text types have been created and added on the entity type 'person'.

5.2 Word

Within the description of relationship type, entity type and attribute type names we use words (nouns or verbs), some of which may have importance as 'key' words, that is, words by which we wish to find elements in the model because they represent a concept which occurs frequently. For example:

- Overtime
- Pay-week
- Person
- Paid
- Pay.

As the key word can be used by more than one 'element' and the description of the element may contain

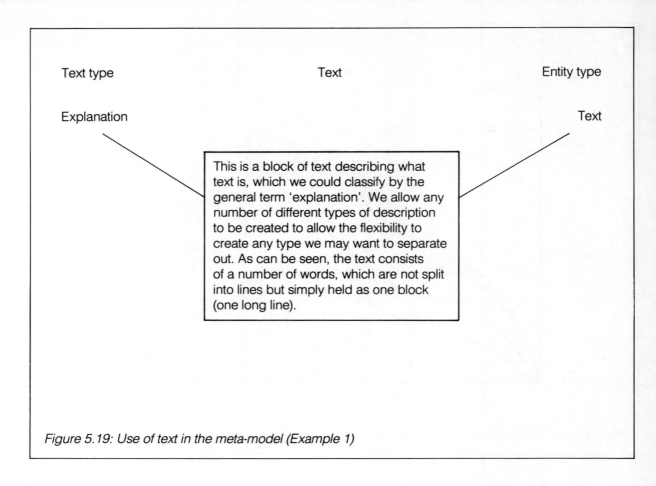

Figure 5.19: Use of text in the meta-model (Example 1)

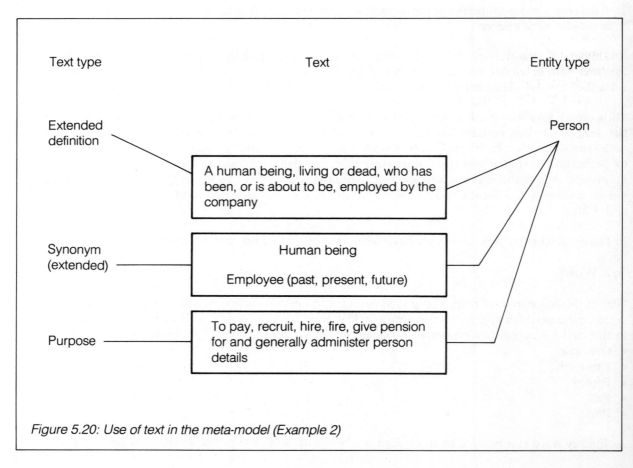

Figure 5.20: Use of text in the meta-model (Example 2)

more than one key word, we show 'usage'. This describes whether the word is 'in context' (in the name) or 'out of context' (not in the name but implied or within the description).

6 General

It can be seen that every concept and 'deliverable' is describable using an entity model which could, in turn, be used to produce a designed system—an advanced data dictionary or *system engine*. This summary completes the description of the facts which have to be collected during entity or data analysis.

Optionality: synonymous with optional.

Organisation design: the task in the SDC whereby activities are grouped into jobs (human) and an organisation is formulated to support those jobs.

Organisation planning: the task of deciding how an organisation, or its jobs, should be changed.

Overview analysis: an analysis, the objective of which, is to provide an overview of a 'project area' or phase. The analysis should be sufficiently detailed to enable the feasibility of various solutions to business problems to be determined and, furthermore, enable the initial scope to be further broken down into priority areas.

Overview model: the model produced at the end of the overview stage of analysis within the SDC.

P

Partitioning: the organisational level/unit at which the population of an entity type permanently divides, such that all the entities outside each population group are of no interest to the organisational units other than that for which the partition was formed.

Permanent attribute type: an attribute type used by more than one activity.

Permanent entity type: an entity type used by more than one activity.

Permitted range: a shorthand way of writing every permitted value. All values within the range, including the delimiting values, are valid values within the format identified for that attribute type.

Permitted value: one of the *valid* values of an attribute type. Normally it is synonymous with the attribute, but where the attribute has been coded the permitted value is the code. The meaning of the code is then the attribute.

Phase: a collection of data analysis deliverables (entity types, relationship types, attribute types and so on) and activity analysis deliverables (activity, event and so on), which together form a 'unit' of the business which merits further study. The choice is based on priorities for study and present problems.

Physical file: a defined area of space on an actual physical storage device.

Planning: the task in the SDC which sets the scope for subsequent study and defines time limits, budget manning and all other factors which ensure that the next stage is completed successfully.

Physical data model: the collection of deliverables produced at the construction stage of the SDC which relate to how the 'logical' (more correctly the design) data model is physically implemented onto storage media. More correctly termed the construction data model.

Primary attribute type: synonymous with basic attribute type.

Q

Quantitative value: a numeric value; a numeric attribute. An attribute which is expressed using numbers and, optionally, decimal points and a sign.

R

Record: an occurrence of a record type.

Record element: synonymous with data element.

Record type: a collection of data items in a predefined sequence which are stored and accessed together as a unit. A logical unit of input.

Relationship: an association between two entities which is always expressed as a verb and is of interest to the enterprise as information because it is required by the activities. In everyday use, this term has been shortened to 'relation'. The analyst should ensure that he is aware which conventions are being followed.

Relationship occurrence: synonymous with relationship.

Relationship type: a classification of relationships based on the entities' classification into entity types and the verb which is being used to describe each relationship.

Responsibility: the jobs (DP or otherwise) which have responsibility for keeping the deliverables up to date. Included within the definition is the access authorisation for the deliverables.

S

Scope: see *Phase.*

SDC: Systems Development Cycle.

SE: see *Software evaluation.*

Segment: synonymous with record type.

Segment type: synonymous with record type.

Set: a type of association between two or more record types which provides a means of access from one record type to the other(s).

Software: a collection of computer code, record types, file types and so on—the means by which data and a number of activities are implemented. Software can be the designed and constructed solution to a business- or a DP-related area.

Software evaluation: the stage in the SDC where software is evaluated for fit against a requirement.

Solution: synonymous with version.

Specific attribute type: an attribute type which describes only one entity type.

Standard name: the name by which something is most commonly known.

Strategic analysis: the analysis which is performed at the strategy stage of the SDC. Its objective is to produce all the deliverables required to formulate a strategy for further development.

Strategy study: a term which groups together all the tasks at the strategic stage of a study—strategic analysis, planning, hardware planning, software evaluation and organisation evaluation. The objective of the strategy study is to identify the prime direction which each of these aspects should be taking—that is, which major hardware, which prime software, which systems?

Subject group: synonymous with aggregate.

Synonym: a word which describes exactly the same thing as another word. Another name for the same thing.

System (designed): a collection of mechanisms which represent a specific method (or way) of achieving an objective. It is possible that more than one way exists to achieve an objective, in which case more than one system will exist.

System (logical and conceptual): a collection of activity and data analysis deliverables which represent one way (or method) of achieving an objective. Unlike a version, different 'systems' can co-exist in any company.

Systems engine: a meta-model, but one used to drive the development process. An active (as opposed to passive) part of the SDC.

T

Timeliness: a measure of how up to date the data is.

Transient attribute types: an attribute type used by only one (elementary) activity.

Transient entity type: an entity type used by only one (elementary) activity.

V

Value range: a contiguous set of permitted values which is expressed by stating only the lowest and highest values in the set.

Version: a collection of data analysis and activity analysis deliverables which represent the solution or the way a business objective can be, or is, achieved. Possible and actual solutions are included within the definition. The difference between a system and a version is that systems can co-exist, versions cannot. Versions represent alternative ways from which either a choice must be made or there must be a transfer from one method to another.

Volumes: the number of entities of a given type.

Volumes at a level: the number of entities of a given type at the organisational level at which partitioning occurs. If a natural split of the entities occurs between different parts of an organisation, the volumes are recorded at this level. If another part of the organisation requires the whole population this is ignored, as the total volumes can be derived from the partitions which have occurred in the population.